PATIENT, EMPOWER THYSELF!

PATIENT, EMPOWER THYSELF!

A New Paradigm for Facing Chaos
and Finding Peace in Healthcare

Claudia Cometa, PharmD

Patient, Empower Thyself

© 2025 by Claudia Cometa, PharmD

All rights reserved. No portion of this publication may be reproduced, stored in a retrieval system, or transmitted by any means—electronic, mechanical, photocopying, recording, or any other—except for brief quotations in printed reviews, without the prior written permission of the publisher.

Library of Congress Control Number: 2024908377

ISBN: 978-1954676893 (paperback)   978-1954676909 (ebook)

Although this publication is designed to provide accurate information about the subject matter, the publisher and the author assume no responsibility for any errors, inaccuracies, omissions, or inconsistencies herein. This publication is intended as a resource; however, it is not intended as a replacement for direct and personalized professional services.

Editors: Jorge David Remy, Dianna Graveman
Cover and Interior Design: Emma Elzinga

Printed in the United States of America

First Edition

3 West Garden Street, Ste. 718
Pensacola, FL 32502
www.indigoriverpublishing.com

Ordering Information:

Quantity sales: Special discounts are available on quantity purchases by corporations, associations, and others. For details, contact the publisher at the address above.

Orders by US trade bookstores and wholesalers: Please contact the publisher at the address above.

With Indigo River Publishing, you can always expect great books, strong voices, and meaningful messages. Most importantly, you'll always find . . . *words worth reading.*

CONTENTS

For my dad, who colored my world by loving unconditionally, living unassumingly, and laughing unapologetically.

INTRODUCTION

HEALTH.

That one word can elicit many different emotions.

For some, it may represent strength and joy.

For others, it may be more indicative of pain and struggle.

In addition to being emotionally charged, it's often an all-or-nothing phenomenon.

We are either not thinking about it at all because our health is in check, or we are all-consumed by a recent diagnosis. Once we find ourselves in the *all-in* camp, we usually stay there out of fear. Fear of our health worsening. Fear of losing our life as we know it.

My parents, sister, and I spent little to no time talking about health for the majority of my life. Our family members mostly felt well, and we experienced few medical challenges. No one in my family was medically trained or worked in the healthcare system in any capacity, so health and healthcare were low on the list of topics at the dining room table.

My husband and I, however, frequently discussed health, in the context of healthcare, in our home. I graduated in 2003 with my doctor of pharmacy degree, and my husband graduated in 2007 with his doctor of medicine degree. Our lives were all-consumed by providing medical care for others in our respective capacities.

Professionally, we were *all-in*.

Personally, however, we were in the *nothing* camp. Cozy, wrapped in a blanket, sipping coffee without a health-related worry in the world.

Then my father showed me a lump in his neck a few months before my husband and I were scheduled to move across the country. My husband, the physician, educated me on the statistical likelihood that this lump would be diagnosed as cancer.

I wanted nothing more than his years of education and training to be wrong. But he was right. The lump was an inflamed lymph node. The diagnosis was squamous cell carcinoma of the neck.

I immediately put my metaphorical coffee down, threw my figurative cozy blanket aside, and entered the *all-in* camp. Health as I knew it was suddenly gone. The future was uncertain. Comfort and complacency were quickly replaced with fear and endless action.

Research. Questions. Doctors' appointments. More research. More questions.

We were quickly thrust into all things *oncology*.

My father responded well to the prescribed radiation and low-dose chemotherapy and was later told he was in remission. The timeline of uncertainty and risk for recurrence was five years, so my father was hyper-focused on this and aware that every day he was inching closer to year number five.

Year five arrived. And with it came an ER visit for severe abdominal pain, which was determined to be due to a ruptured and bleeding spleen. This relatively rare condition was a result of his spleen being under pressure from cancer, follicular lymphoma to be exact.

We were right back where we started, different details, different cancer. However, we never left the *all-in* camp once we joined. With every scan, lab work, and office visit following cancer number one, we held our collective breath.

I personally began evaluating everything I consumed, both through my mouth and my mind, for its potential to push me over the cancer edge as well. I read every story in print that detailed another person's cancer journey. Because we were all suddenly connected.

My father passed away on April 15, 2017, a year almost to the day from his lymphoma diagnosis. As the only member of the immediate family with a healthcare background, I was his primary advocate throughout both cancer journeys. My clinical pharmacy background set me up perfectly for the most important role I never expected to face.

I attended every medical appointment, reviewed every lab and imaging report, and communicated with all the physicians. I monitored my dad's online portal and answered all his questions. I was his personal medical concierge, and I was honored to hold this title.

What I discovered during my time advocating for my dad was that the medical system I had worked in since 2003 was, and is, broken. Not just sprained or strained. It's broken. Shattered. In many pieces.

I discovered countless errors during my father's journey. His weight was erroneously documented as almost double his actual weight. Medical records indicated physical examinations that were never actually performed. Due to this suboptimal care, I fired two hospital systems and several individual physicians along the way. I was shocked and disappointed by the lack of compassion, poor communication, and difficulty in navigating the complicated system for the average person without a healthcare degree.

I looked around at the ICU rooms surrounding my dad's, and I wondered who was helping the other patients. Who was monitoring their labs? Who was asking their physicians the difficult questions?

The apparent answer: no one.

I couldn't bear the thought. So I made the only decision I could—I would do for others what I did for my dad. Since 2017, I have helped many clients navigate the healthcare system and find the answers they need. I am *all-in*. On my health. My family's health. And my clients' health. This *all-in* camp is no longer filled with fear for me. It's filled with hope. Hope for a new approach to health and wellness.

I wrote this book from the perspective of both sides of the healthcare landscape—employee and patient. I have an intimate understanding of how the system works. And I now have a similarly intimate understanding of the patient experience.

The journey here wasn't easy or linear. But I have been able to find peace along the way by identifying the tangible and intangible factors that are in my control and releasing my tight grip on the others. I wrote this book to help you do the same. To help you go *all-in* on *your* health, while replacing fear with hope and worry with peace.

Real stories of both family members and clients emphasize and expand upon the concepts presented. All names have been changed to maintain confidentiality.

At the end of each chapter, Peace Points help summarize the content in a way that leaves you less stressed than when you started. Guided meditations included in some chapters help you dive further into those concepts that might take a bit more time and attention to master. To listen to the audio version of the guided meditations, visit https://claudiacometa.com/book-meditations/.

This is a journey, my friends. And *Patient, Empower Thyself!* is your guide on that journey to establish a new paradigm, a new way of thinking about both your health and your healthcare. A guide accompanies and mentors, leads and offers advice. A guide is not intended to be your directive or prescription for any specific choices regarding your health. I envision this book being the opposite of a to-do checklist. In other words, I hope to teach you *how* to think rather than *what* to think. If I am successful, you will finish the book with a deeper understanding of the medical system, a heightened confidence in navigating your own care, and a new level of curiosity and questioning that will leave you empowered.

My goal is to honor the diversity of readers and experiences, with the hope you'll explore and identify the path that aligns with your individual needs and goals. And hopefully you'll discover that the *all-in* camp can be a beautiful destination.

CHAPTER 1

SYSTEM

Forming a historical perspective and understanding physician training/practice culture is crucial to navigating the healthcare world.

Historical Journey Through the US Medical System

THE healthcare system is overly, and arguably unnecessarily, complex and broken.

While I, like many of you, would love to wave a magic wand and fix it, it's unfortunately not that easy. Many individuals and organizations are putting forth their best effort to simplify and streamline parts of the system that simply aren't working. Recently, large tech enterprises like Amazon have decided to don their own armor and step into the arena. In addition to acquiring the online pharmacy PillPack and rebranding to Amazon Pharmacy, the retail giant launched its own telehealth platform, Amazon Clinic. Time will tell if this will result in positive, negative, or neutral effects on the overall system.

While we watch this play out and hope for impactful change, it's important to have a historical understanding of how we got here. I am not a historian and have no intention to bore any of you who might feel similarly, so I will keep this section concise and, as the medical community says, "high-yield."

The first formal US medical school was founded in 1765 at the College of Philadelphia (Custers 2018).[1] Regulation was lacking, and many students gained their knowledge and skills as apprentices through the middle of the nineteenth century.

At the end of the nineteenth century, medical schools required between two and three years of formal training, with few textbooks and irregular testing of material. In 1942, the Liaison Committee on Medical Education was born and began to change the landscape of undergraduate medical education requirements. Clinical training, or post-graduate medical education, first began to face regulation in 1980 with the creation of the Accreditation Council for Graduate Medical Education (ACGME).

While medical education was undergoing a significant evolution, so was medical practice.

Many of you reading this may have heard of doctors making "house calls" several decades ago. In the current post-pandemic setting of masked office visits and telemedicine, it is hard to imagine a physician coming to physically treat you in the comfort of your home. And for good reason.

This medical practice was common in the early 1900s, well before anyone reading this was born (Moseley 2008).[2] At that time, people paid out of pocket for medical care, health insurance didn't exist, and physicians and hospitals both lacked regulation. Modern medicine as we know it came to the scene in 1910, around the same time that surgery for common conditions became a regular practice.

The American Medical Association (AMA) began its regulation

---

1   Custers and Cate, "The History of Medical Education," S51.

2   Moseley, "The U.S. Health Care Non-System," 324.

between 1900–1910. In 1913, hospitals faced the first accrediting body, the American College of Surgeons. Insurance companies then entered the scene, with over twenty plans available by 1937. Before the middle of the century, President Truman proposed a program to provide national health insurance; however, the AMA felt so strongly against it they called it a "communist plot."

From 1950 on, significant change occurred rapidly. Medications, vaccines, and organ transplants became options for the public. The health insurance sector quickly multiplied to over seven hundred companies. In 1965, Medicare and Medicaid were introduced. Five years later, the concept of "health maintenance organizations" (HMOs) was born. Healthcare spending increased exponentially in the latter part of the 1900s due to costly technologies and continues to the present day.

From this brief history of both the healthcare system and medical education in the US, one can see a pattern emerge. Few to no regulations result in lesser-trained physicians who practice freely as they feel is best without oversight by governing bodies or commercial payors. More regulations lead to heightened educational standards with less freedom in clinical practice and more interference from insurance companies.

Of additional importance is the focus shift in medical education that coincides with the post-1950s boom in medication and technological advancements. As of 2021, there were over twenty thousand prescription drugs approved for marketing (FDA 2021).[3] In addition, most all disease states are now treated based on a clinical practice guideline created by an authority in the field, typically a medical association dedicated to the associated specialty. Guidelines are created to do what their title suggests—guide. However, they are often viewed and used as more of an evidence-based standard against which non-following physicians are questioned and scrutinized. We can begin to understand how the priority of medical education has shifted from anatomy and physiology to surgical techniques and to the current curriculum, which emphasizes

---

3   "FDA at a Glance," 1.

pharmacology and guideline-directed, medication-based treatments for various medical conditions.

In addition, numerous studies have shown an insufficient number of hours dedicated to nutrition in medical education (Crowley 2019).[4] Anecdotally, I can confirm firsthand from physicians I know that most medical schools do not prioritize nutrition as a topic worthy of discussion or training. As a result, to no fault of their own, new physicians are exiting medical school ready to implement what they've been taught—specifically to prescribe a medication for every ailment—and with a lack of understanding of how nutrition impacts our health.

Medical Culture

Now that we have a baseline understanding of the historical timeline of physician education and practice environment, our next layer to add in is the medical culture. With my husband being a physician and our relationship spanning more than three decades, I have witnessed the internal hierarchical culture firsthand. I've also spoken to countless colleagues and read several books written by physicians that confirm my observations.

Physicians experience multiple layers of inferiority and superiority throughout their training. As premedical students, they realize they are at the bottom of the ecosystem food chain. Their role is to achieve stellar grades, excel in the required standardized tests, and shadow as many physicians as possible to earn letters of recommendation. They hold zero power and must impress those who do. For those who pass this stage and receive an acceptance to medical school, the temporary excitement of this achievement is quickly dissipated.

The rigors of medical education and stress over grades and more standardized tests become quickly overwhelming. The students are keenly aware of the competitive nature of residency placement looming

---

4   Crowley, Ball, and Hiddink, "Nutrition in Medical Education," e379–89.

in their future and feel an endless need to excel. For those who graduate medical school and earn grades high enough to be granted a residency spot, which by the way is not guaranteed, the official title of *doctor* feels gratifying.

But not for long.

First-year residents are called *interns* and are treated accordingly. Interns are assigned all the grunt work and face frequent quizzes on their knowledge, with the usual intention of highlighting their inferior understanding of medicine compared to their superior attending physicians.

Once they complete their intern year, they arrive at the next stage and earn the title *resident*. They celebrate their rise in the food chain and proceed as they have been taught, specifically passing on the undesirable tasks to the new interns below them to ensure the interns know their place.

And the cultural rules, and roles, continue.

Far from being out of the woods, residents continue to be pressed by their superiors on medical knowledge and now face the life-altering decision ahead—seek additional training as a fellow or accept a competitive disadvantage by finding non-fellowship-trained employment.

Those who enter the work force directly after residency training and seek a position with a private practice find themselves quickly dropping back down in the new hierarchy—the world of the practicing physician.

As newbies fresh out of training, they now have to prove themselves to their partners, clinic or hospital staff, and patients. Their medical school education and residency training, while acknowledged, holds little value or meaning until they demonstrate their clinical skills in the proverbial trenches. They often are assigned longer working hours, more nights and weekends on call, and additional volunteer duties they quietly take on to avoid rocking any boats.

If this sounds brutal, that's because, to most of us, it is.

While many of us are familiar with the hierarchy of professional advancement in a variety of fields, the nuances are a bit different and more complex when the work involves caring for a human life. There is no widely accepted milestone or medical knowledge landmark that officially identifies a physician as an expert.

In the academia setting, a colleague or superior may measure a physician's value by the number of published articles in peer-reviewed journals. In a private practice clinical role, that measure may be years of experience or documented clinical outcomes.

There are a multitude of good reasons why only approximately one quarter of 1 percent of the US population is doctors. I just laid out a small fraction of them. Why do I share all of this? It's my belief that understanding the medical system from every angle will help you as a patient navigate it more effectively. While the onus shouldn't be on you to figure out this complicated web, proactively doing so will only help you.

Let me give you some real-world examples of how this looks.

How to Use This Insider Information

Imagine you are in an exam room of an academic institution or university-based clinic. It's a teaching hospital, so all of the layers of hierarchy I just described are active and in play. A young woman knocks on the door and enters the exam room. She introduces herself as Dr. Jones, and her badge confirms her role: PHYSICIAN. You find her demeanor to be shaky and lacking confidence. She asks you a barrage of questions, which feels like scripted check boxes to you rather than out-of-the box thinking. She finishes her exam and questioning, then excuses herself to talk to her attending physician.

Because you have read this book, you know what's happening behind the scenes. Dr. Jones is either an intern or a resident (possibly a fellow, but the point is the same). Assuming she is an intern, she recently graduated from medical school and is newly experiencing what it's like to be a practicing doctor. She is being handed grunt work by her superiors, working long hours, and is likely being asked a multitude of questions by her attending to prove her place in the hierarchy right now as you sit and wait.

Dr. Jones returns to your room accompanied by her attending physician, Dr. Lopez. With quickness and confidence, Dr. Lopez asks you a few pointed questions, which you realize should have been asked earlier. You see Dr. Jones hold her head down, embarrassed that she missed these key points. Dr. Lopez hands you a prescription and sends you on your way.

How does your understanding of the medical culture and this specific interplay help you personally? You realize Dr. Jones' lack of confidence is due to a lack of experience. Rather than feeling frustrated, you use this hierarchical understanding to your advantage. When considering to whom you should direct your list of prepared questions, you choose to wait for the attending physician rather than ask Dr. Jones.

You understand that your appointments in an academic setting like this will almost always take longer, so you prepare for that. You decide that any follow-up questions after the visit should be directed to Dr. Lopez, and if they are answered by Dr. Jones, you will express your gratitude but seek confirmation. You have compassion for the rigorous and difficult training she continues to endure, but you ultimately seek confident responses to your medical questions.

On the other hand, if the academic setting and multitude of hierarchical figures is not something you wish to experience again, you will know to seek a private practice physician instead.

Furthermore, knowing how the landscape of medical education has changed over recent decades, you expect the treatment offered by your physician to be a medication or procedure. Or possibly multiple. It's unlikely, based on the lack of training provided in medical school, that your physician will offer you advice on nutrition, movement, or alternative treatment modalities. You realize your physician's inability or unwillingness to consult on these topics does not equate to their lack of importance. It's simply a reflection of the priorities of the medical school curriculum in this country. Therefore, you acknowledge the basis for your consultant physician's advice and decide as a consultee whether to seek additional assistance to further address your health concerns. Note: this shift in language that includes consultant and consultee will be explained more in Chapter 5: Unlearning.

Your deep understanding of the medical culture allows you to manage additional expectations. If your clinic appointment is late in the day, say 4:40 p.m., it's likely your physician is behind, and your wait time will be longer. It's also probable that your doctor is exhausted after working all day, potentially since the prior evening. The seemingly endless medical charting ahead, as well as family members waiting at home for dinner, overloads your physician's mental capacity, leaving little attentiveness for addressing your concerns. Rather than being frustrated and wanting the system to be different, you realize that's not a good use of your time or energy and instead plan your appointments early in the day.

The medical hierarchy also plays a significant role in hospital settings, requiring even more of your self-advocacy and awareness. Residencies begin across the nation on July 1 with few exceptions. And while this may seem like unnecessary information for you to know, it's quite the opposite. If your preferred hospital is a teaching institution, the benefits of which we will discuss soon, finding yourself hospitalized in July often means you will be cared for by an intern or resident.

While they are medical doctors and have earned that title, you are aware of what is happening behind the scenes. The intern, a.k.a. the physician on your team with the least experience, is being given the grunt work and is likely tasked with ordering your medications and treatments. The intern may have just learned the electronic medical record system at the hospital a week ago during orientation.

As such, the potential for errors when entering a medication order in the system is relatively high. The pharmacists receiving the order are a secondary check, but not a guaranteed source of error identification and resolution.

This may feel like a losing scenario, but I hope you know by now that I would never leave you feeling hopeless and helpless.

Similar to the scenarios above, your understanding of the hospital system can now help you navigate your care. You realize your team includes all members of the hierarchy, and you are more frequently visited by the intern or resident than the attending. When your nurse hands you a new medication you have not yet seen, you know to ask what it is and what it's for because, well, July. You wait to see the attending to ask your nonurgent medical questions rather than trusting the intern or resident. If you were told you need imaging, such as a CT or MRI, and days have passed since that has been mentioned, you realize it's possible the intern or resident forgot to order it. Rather than assume you no longer need it, you know to ask the team or the nurse to follow up.

Because, July.

I know what you may be thinking. It's unreasonable that anyone should have to exert this much oversight on their care. Why can't the system just do what needs to be done in a timely manner without errors? Trust me, I understand and don't disagree.

If screaming this from the rooftop would help fix the system, I would be voiceless by now. What I have learned in my life journey is that acceptance of reality doesn't have to equate with agreement or approval. We can accept that the system is broken, because it is, yet not approve of the ways in which it is broken. Resisting this truth or wanting it to be different only serves to enhance our struggle and take energy away from healing.

Please understand this doesn't mean we should accept or approve of mediocre or suboptimal care. Medical malpractice attorneys will be among the first to tell you that you aren't without rights, including the right to seek justice if your physician was negligent. What I am suggesting is to use your new understanding of the current system realities, as unfortunate as they are, to more effectively navigate your care and use your voice.

This topic of acceptance over approval is so important I believe it deserves a real-life example. When my dad was diagnosed with lymphoma and we were thrust headfirst into the medical system, I was quick to put on my fighting gloves. When I found out the pulmonology fellow, which you will recall is the next hierarchical step above resident, inaccurately documented that my dad's lungs were "clear to auscultation," I was angry. In medical jargon, this indicates he listened to my dad's chest with a stethoscope and heard no concerning sounds. He never did, however, listen to my dad's chest, and a few days later, my dad needed a chest tube to drain excess fluid around his lungs. How could this happen?

How could a physician in his last year of training document an untruth in the medical chart? How could he specialize in lungs, yet not do a proper physical exam on that organ that could have prevented my dad from needing a painful chest tube? I know exactly how it happened.

Charting in electronic medical record systems is tedious. To help time efficiency, the technical staff often helps the clinical staff create note templates. These templates auto-populate commonly used statements and require the physician to edit the statements that are inaccurate. One can imagine how this process is ripe with error potential and highlights the advances and setbacks of overreliance on technological automation. "It was like that last time, so this tracks."

I wanted the entire office staff to know how angry I was. I wanted to change the whole system in that moment to prevent it from happening again. But that wasn't possible or realistic. It also wasn't possible for me to will this situation to not have happened. Instead, I brought it to the attention of my dad's attending physician and used what I knew of the system and its inherent error potential to continue to monitor his medical records for additional errors, of which there were many.

Where the System Is Headed

There is some good news in the midst of these unfortunate truths. Many compassionate, kind-hearted souls are working hard to fix the healthcare system. Some are physicians who desperately want to return to quality patient care while also maintaining a sustainable life balance for themselves and their families. Others are wealthy businesspeople with a desire to use their financial leverage to change the system they too need to utilize. I personally welcome with open arms whomever is willing to step into this arena and fight for positive change.

Many improvements have already been implemented and are permanently changing the healthcare landscape for the better, in my opinion. Direct Primary Care (DPC) is a newer practice and payment model that combines the attentiveness of yesteryear with the technology of today. Physicians and other providers who adopt this model charge a reasonable flat monthly fee to their patients. In return, they offer close to 24/7 availability for any health concerns that may arise. Their patient volumes are a small fraction of what is common in conventional primary care practices, and their lack of involvement with insurance companies removes an often-disruptive middle man from the relationship.

While this model does not suggest that medical insurance will soon become a commodity of the past, it does highlight an important shift. Patients and physicians alike are seeking ways to more deeply nurture a relationship that has suffered under the directives and regulations of the insurance industry. Patients are slowly feeling more seen and heard. And DPC physicians are breathing a sigh of relief as they focus on patient-centered care, lower their administrative burdens, and ultimately realign with their goal of quality over quantity.

In addition, patient advocacy is a field that has grown exponentially, largely out of necessity. Institutions have created advocate positions to help patients navigate complex areas such as oncology care. Independent patient advocates, such as myself, have also come to the scene. Due to being self-employed, they remove any conflict of interest and are able to solely focus on the interests and goals of the client. This large network of change-makers includes individuals with expertise in medical guidance, insurance billing, preventative wellness, and more.

Also, while some hospitals are leaning more into technology and away from personalized care, others are taking a more progressive approach and incorporating more integrative approaches to healing.

Many people don't realize that not all hospitals are created equal. Small, rural community hospitals usually don't attract physicians at the height of their careers. As such, staffing and resources are sometimes so low that telehealth services are used in critical areas, including the ICU.

Yes, you read that right.

An intensivist will see you, but only through a computer screen while you have a tube in your throat. This is one reason why choosing a larger teaching hospital is often preferred. Another reason is the academic movement towards incorporating alternative healing modalities, including chair yoga, meditation, canine visits, and healing through the arts.

We are moving the needle, my friends. Slowly, but surely. But until a utopian system is created, I hope you feel better-equipped to use your newly acquired knowledge to speak up for yourself or a loved one. Breathe in acceptance of reality; breathe out hope and self-advocacy.

Peace Points

- Use your understanding of the changing medical landscape to help you more effectively navigate the journey.

- Work on accepting the reality of the current broken system, while maintaining a desire for improvement.

- Find hope in the improvements already in place and consider whether these approaches may be helpful options for you as you heal.

CHAPTER 2

TRUST

Shifts in our healthcare landscape have become fuel for public distrust. There are many opportunities to rebuild this trust, from the individual level to policy reform.

TRUST: To believe in the reliability, truth, ability, or strength of. My dad trusted the medical system without hesitation or question. As a previous employee of the same system, I also jumped into this journey with a high level of trust. Our approaches in utilizing that trust, however, were slightly different. My dad nodded his head during appointments, while I took notes to ultimately trust but verify later. If a physician reported a specific statistic or treatment guideline, I made it a point to confirm or deny the accuracy of what was stated.

Throughout history, the most trusted members of society have been those who are seen as acting in the best interests of the community. These individuals and groups also have a demonstrated track record of competence, expertise, and ethical behavior.

Teachers and educators are often seen as playing a critical role in shaping the minds and values of future generations. Law enforcement officers, firefighters, and other first responders are also often viewed as trustworthy by the public as they protect and serve their communities.

Healthcare professionals have historically been a trusted group due to their role in caring for people's health and well-being. Their extensive training and expertise have heightened their trustworthiness in the eyes of the public.

Our ability or willingness to trust others is impacted by a variety of factors. For those who have experienced betrayal by loved ones or been a victim of criminal activity, trusting other people can be a seemingly impossible task. Even for those whose childhood and adult experiences were otherwise positive, the present-day realities of the healthcare system can serve as its own fuel for creating distrust.

Trust in the Healthcare System

As we established in Chapter 1, gone are the days when the physician came to the home for a lengthy visit to evaluate the patient and his environment. In its place, we face cold, sterile exam rooms filled with computer screens and clocks reminding us, and the staff, that our time there, and their attention to us, is limited.

The shifting landscape of the medical system is further highlighted by the frequency with which medications are prescribed for most every ailment. Despite the famous Greek physician Hippocrates being quoted as saying, "Let food be thy medicine and let thy medicine be food," it is a rare physician who would take this approach to illness today.

The US pharmaceutical industry is the largest in the world, including research and development, marketing, and profits. This industry has found itself under scrutiny for focusing on profits at the expense of patient welfare. The commonly used term "Big Pharma" is believed to have emerged in the 1970s by consumer advocates and critics of the industry who were concerned about its growing influence.

Adding to the public distrust, many pharmaceutical companies have been found to engage in unethical and illegal practices, such as marketing drugs for unapproved uses or downplaying risks associated with their medications.

One might hypothesize, based on personal experience or reports in the media, that trust in the current healthcare system is relatively low. Throughout and following the COVID-19 pandemic, this distrust grew at heightened levels due to misinformation, conflicting reports, and a lack of agreement among healthcare professionals on appropriate treatments and approach.

To quantify the public's trust, or lack thereof, in the US healthcare system, the American Board of Internal Medicine Foundation commissioned NORC at the University of Chicago to survey the general public as well as physicians on this topic (NORC 2021).[5] Key findings from 2,069 adults showed that trust in physicians did indeed decrease during the pandemic, but trust in individual clinicians remained higher than in the healthcare system as a whole. The primary driver of individual physician distrust was too little time spent with them as patients.

Among the 600 physicians surveyed, almost all said that spending an appropriate amount of time with patients is important. Yet, a quarter of patients said physicians do not spend a sufficient amount of time with them. One-third of physicians experienced a decreased level of trust in the healthcare system during the pandemic. In addition, only half of physicians said they trust healthcare leaders and executives.

This tangible glimpse into our medical system is in alignment with my personal and professional experience. All of my clients have at least one physician they feel doesn't spend enough time with them. In addition, almost all of them have verbalized some level of distrust in the healthcare system and/or in individual physicians.

And none of my clients wish they were taking more medications.

Jennifer established care with a new cardiologist. During the first appointment, he spent ample time listening to her and reviewing her medical records. We were off to a good start. At subsequent appointments, however, he asked questions he had asked at prior appointments

---

5   NORC, "Surveys of Trust in the U.S. Health Care System."

and to which she previously provided answers. Jennifer found herself repeating important medical details she felt should have been documented in her chart.

Her trust in this physician began to decrease with time. And I didn't blame her. While I don't expect physicians to remember every detail discussed at appointments, a pattern over time of information being lost or disregarded is fuel for distrust.

It is important to note that not all patients struggle with trust in this way. In fact, my father had an unwavering trust in every member of his healthcare team. Even when they provided him with justification to question this trust, he found a way to stay the course.

Surely they had good reason to document his weight as three hundred pounds when he actually weighed 175 pounds on a good day. And there *must* have been justification behind his pulmonologist documenting that he listened to his failing lungs when in reality, he did not.

Thankfully, he had me by his side to navigate these errors and missteps, allowing him to remain mostly at peace throughout the journey. Many people, however, find themselves walking through the muddy waters of the healthcare system alone, desperately seeking to find answers.

From people they can trust.

Trust in Yourself

The concept of trust is multifaceted.

While our trust in the healthcare system is affected by many internal and external variables, trust in ourselves also plays a significant role in our health journey. It can feel unfamiliar and possibly even uncomfortable to turn the trust conversation around, but this self-awareness can be powerful.

The confidence and belief in our ability and capacity to achieve a goal is also known as self-efficacy. In other words, do you trust in yourself?

When relating to our health, these questions would sound like:

Do you trust in your ability to manage your health?

Do you trust in your ability to engage in and sustain an exercise routine?

Do you believe you can maintain a healthy diet?

When applying this to everyday scenarios, it might sound like:

Are you confident you can skip dessert even if your family has cake?

Do you trust in your ability to avoid smoking if you are around others who regularly smoke?

If we take this further into navigating the healthcare system, it would sound like:

Do you believe you can prepare for your appointments and ask your physician difficult questions?

Do you trust in your capacity to seek a second opinion if you feel your physician's opinion might not be accurate? (Note: we will dive deeper into the concept of opinion in Chapter 5.)

This concept has garnered much interest in the medical field. In fact, a survey was developed and is in use to assess an individual's self-efficacy. Researchers have used this when studying the impact of self-efficacy on health outcomes.

In one study of over eight hundred primary care patients with multiple diagnoses, researchers found that those with higher disease burden had lower self-efficacy scores (Peters et al. 2019).[6] In other words, the sicker participants had a lesser level of confidence in their ability to manage their health. These patients also had an associated lower quality of life.

It is evident from this study and others that the amount of personal control we expect to have over our behaviors impacts our health.

---

6   Peters et al., "Self-Efficacy and Health-Related Quality of Life," 4–6.

How to Rebuild Trust

Based on my countless interactions with physicians, I believe they want to spend more time with their patients. They understand the concept of quality over quantity, and they realize true impact requires time. However, the business of medicine has created a culture of prioritizing volume, which undoubtedly has played a role in the distrust physicians now have in their own leaders and executives.

With the culture of distrust starting at the executive level and trickling down, the challenges and struggles can feel overwhelming. Hope for change and progress can feel futile. While I don't believe we are headed back to the days of house calls and paper medical charts, I do believe we can rebuild the levels of trust that existed during that time.

As I hope I have outlined in the preceding chapters, becoming an activated and engaged patient is of paramount importance. This is not to say, in any way, that the onus to rebuild trust in the healthcare system lies solely on patients. That could not be further from the truth. But I do believe effective progress starts with each individual changing what is within control.

In fact, patient engagement is a two-way street. It requires that the providers involve their patients in care planning and goal setting. It also requires that patients prepare to be engaged during their visits, providing their physicians with the information needed to make the most educated decisions about their care.

This patient-centered approach to care involves shared decision-making and feedback about the entire care experience.

You may be thinking: This sounds great, but how do I persuade my physician to adopt an approach centered on me? How do I encourage this type of engagement and ultimately help to rebuild the trust in our patient-physician relationship?

Communicate Your Wishes and Goals

Explain to your physician that you would like to improve your relationship and rapport by increasing engagement on both sides. Discuss your plans to be more involved in your care and better prepared for visits. And in return, ask for enhanced communication and a shared approach to decision-making.

If you find, after a few subsequent visits, your requests have gone unheard or unnoticed, I give you full permission to consider changing physicians. And if leaving that practice is your next step, you will do so feeling confident you did everything in your power to make it work.

If your self-efficacy, or trust in yourself, is relatively low, you can build this trust by performing small steps. For example, if your goal is to exercise daily and you currently exercise once a week, start by increasing your goal one day at a time. After you're consistent with two days a week, increase to three. With each increase, your self-efficacy increases through personal accomplishment.

Another approach to increasing self-efficacy is to observe others. Brenda, a client of mine, had a deep distrust in both the medical system and her capacity to effectively interact with her medical team. This distrust arose from a longstanding history of being treated poorly by physicians and nurses.

Brenda asked me to attend her appointments via speakerphone so I could step in if the conversation became difficult or she didn't understand what was being said. She did not feel confident in her ability to respond in these scenarios and wanted my assistance. During the appointments, she would call out my name when she was ready for me to step in, and I would take over.

In doing so, she would observe my approach and witness the ease with which the physician would respond. This would eventually allow her to increase her confidence to do this on her own.

Beyond the individual level, the healthcare system as a whole has some significant work to do in the quest to rebuild the public's trust.

Improving transparency should not be seen as optional, but rather a necessity. Patients need and deserve clear and accurate information about the services they are receiving. This includes being invited to give adequate informed consent in the form of a discussion, not left to a lengthy form to read and sign. It also includes clarity on policies, procedures, outcomes, and pricing.

A client of mine was advised to wear a portable cardiac device to monitor her heart rate and rhythm at various times of the day. Her physician ordered a specific device that is more expensive than the standard monitor. Although she had justifiable reason to do so, this was not explained to the patient or preapproved through the insurance prior to ordering.

Months later, my client faced a bill over $5,000 due to her insurance company denying this device and stating it is considered "investigational." We ended up appealing this denial and winning, but there was no transparency about the decision to choose this device, the insurance coverage or lack thereof, or the out-of-pocket cost she may face.

Thankfully, pricing transparency has garnered the attention of policy makers. The Transparency in Coverage rule developed by the Centers for Medicare and Medicaid Services (CMS) requires health insurers to disclose pricing for covered services and items. In addition, the Hospital Price Transparency rule requires that each hospital operating in the US provide clear and accessible pricing information online about the items and services they provide.

We are making progress.

Baby steps are still steps.

Our journey to rebuilding trust will also require addressing disparities in access to care and promoting diversity and inclusion. In the previously mentioned NORC survey, Black and Hispanic respondents reported more barriers to adhere to doctors' recommendations. This was also true for those without a college degree and for low-income households.

With attention to increasing access to care in underserved

communities, addressing bias and discrimination in healthcare settings, and promoting cultural sensitivity, our healthcare system can begin to rebuild the trust from these affected groups.

Stephen Covey said it best: "Trust is the glue of life. It's the most essential ingredient in effective communication. It's the foundational principle that holds all relationships."

Peace Points

- Healthcare professionals were once among the most trusted members of society.
- The COVID-19 pandemic negatively impacted the public's trust of the healthcare system as a whole.
- There are many ways we can begin to rebuild our self-efficacy, the physician-patient trust, and trust in healthcare policy.

CHAPTER 3

BELIEF

Our beliefs about our health, the medical system, and our body's ability to heal impact our choices and ultimately the outcomes we experience.

BELIEF is trust, faith, or confidence in someone or something. My dad believed all physicians were superior in knowledge and that their wisdom surpassed his own about his body. He was told by many physicians in the months leading up to his diagnosis that his relatively vague gastrointestinal symptoms were due to the "GI bug going around." The depth of his belief in their knowledge led him to rarely, if ever, question their assessment or plan. In addition, due to his family history of longevity and health, he believed he was blessed with good genetics, and lifestyle factors like exercise were of lesser importance for him.

Our belief systems largely stem from a complicated web of experiences, mentors, cultural influences, and individual inferences. We hold beliefs about religious and existential topics, personal and professional relationship dynamics, financial frugality, and the list goes on and on.

Our beliefs also trickle into our health. Some believe training at an Ivy League medical school and residency program make physicians superior in their specialty. Others believe a compassionate and kind bedside manner is more valuable than academic knowledge. We also hold beliefs about the state of the healthcare system, its ability and willingness to care for us, and the underlying agenda of the corporations who profit most.

Many people hold beliefs about individual treatments and procedures, specifically whether their body will respond positively or negatively. While not largely acknowledged or understood in our modern medical system, the beliefs held by patients and physicians can and do impact the outcomes that are ultimately experienced.

The formation of beliefs within the healthcare system was discussed earlier in Chapter 1, which explores how medical training and culture influences physician beliefs. Ultimately, as I lay out in this chapter, whether we develop beliefs from personal experience or from accepting what others tell us, these beliefs influence our health.

Placebo Effect

In the book *Mind Over Medicine*, author and physician Dr. Lissa Rankin shares countless stories, both case studies in the literature and anecdotal stories from her own practice, that fuel this discussion (Rankin 2020).[7] She references how a cancer patient who was diagnosed with lymphosarcoma in 1957 had exhausted all available treatment options. His physician gave him a prognosis of less than one week after his cancer advanced to his neck, chest, abdomen, spleen, and liver. The patient, desperate to live, learned about an investigational drug that required clinical trial candidates to have a prognosis of at least three months.

He persisted in asking his physician to help him despite his prognostic ineligibility. The physician, who was practicing under a different set of rules and regulations in the 1950s, conceded and provided the patient with the medication as requested. To everyone's shock, the

---

7   Rankin, Mind Over Medicine: Scientific Proof That You Can Heal Yourself.

patient was cancer-free ten days following the dose. Not long after, the American Medical Association reported research that showed the investigational drug was ineffective. After finding out the medication failed to get approved due to its lack of effectiveness in clinical trials, the patient became depressed; his cancer returned, and he ultimately died.

In addition, Dr. Rankin shares a study involving an orthopedic surgeon performing either conventional surgery or sham (fake) surgery on patients with debilitating knee pain. Those receiving the sham surgery still underwent sedation and incisions into the skin to create the belief that conventional surgery took place. What he found was shocking. The same percentage of patients experienced resolution of their knee pain in both groups, approximately 33 percent. At one point in the study, those who had undergone the sham surgery experienced less knee pain than those who had the conventional surgical procedure.

How could this be?

How is it possible that an ineffective drug helped a patient's cancer go into remission? And how can patients who have undergone fake surgery experience relief from their condition to the same extent as those who had actual surgery?

Belief. Trust, faith, or confidence in someone or something.

This phenomenon is not limited to the beliefs of patients. The placebo effect involving physician beliefs has been documented in the literature as well.

In an article published in *Nature Human Behaviour* in October 2019, researchers asked undergraduate students to play the roles of patients and doctors (Chen 2019).[8] They studied the effects of two creams, one identified as placebo and the other named Thermedol. The "doctors" were conditioned to believe Thermedol was superior to placebo in relieving pain. In reality, both creams were simply petroleum jelly with no active pain-relieving ingredients.

Researchers found that across all three experiments, the "patients" reported feeling less pain when the doctors applied the cream they

---

8   Chen et al., "Socially Transmitted Placebo Effects," 1295–1305.

believed was effective, namely Thermedol. This was further validated by skin conductance tests and the facial expressions of the patients. In addition, the patients felt the doctors were more empathetic when they believed the treatment was going to work.

How could petroleum jelly with no active ingredients actually relieve their pain?

Belief. Trust, faith, or confidence in someone or something.

Nocebo Effect

On the flipside of the placebo effect is what is known as the nocebo effect. A nocebo effect occurs when the individual's undesirable expectations of a treatment cause the treatment to have a more negative effect than it would otherwise have. After reading the anecdotal stories of this phenomenon, I began to reflect on my dad's journey.

My father tended to lean on the pessimistic side of life, even before his cancer diagnosis. He was a kind, supportive, hardworking man, but he often defaulted to seeing the glass as half-empty. For reasons that never became clear, my father held a belief he would die at the age of seventy-five. His diagnosis occurred at age seventy-four.

Despite his first set of follow-up scans after his initial chemotherapy regimen, showing possible treatment response, all future scans showed progressive disease seemingly resistant to treatment. His oncologists changed the treatment protocol several times, but each time they expressed their doubts that his lymphoma would be responsive. At our last visit, the oncologist informed us that his cancer had spread to multiple organs and there were no further treatment options. When my dad asked how much time he had left, specifically inquiring if it was at least three months, the oncologist shook his head no.

My dad returned home and judiciously watched the clock. He believed he had less than three months because he had trust, faith, and confidence in his oncologist.

He died approximately two months later at the age of seventy-five, ten days before his seventy-sixth birthday.

Beliefs About the Medical System

The impact of our beliefs isn't limited to medications or surgery. For often justifiable reasons, many people hold negative beliefs about the medical system and its willingness or ability to help them. Since our personal experiences and resulting inferences contribute to our beliefs, one significant or multiple minor adverse interactions with a medical institution or professional can create a blanket belief about the entire healthcare system.

I often find this to be the case with my clients. In our modern medical landscape, it's not a stretch of the imagination that unpleasant experiences occur in emergency departments, lengthy hospital stays, pharmacies, and most all areas of the system. It's often these experiences, and the desire to not repeat them or experience worse, that leads people to contact me.

Confirmation Bias

We as humans have a tendency to seek out and interpret information in a way that supports our beliefs. Regardless of the string of causative events, once we believe that the healthcare system is trying to hurt us, we naturally seek examples that support or confirm this belief.

Mary had a complex medical history that stumped many of her healthcare professionals and led to several diagnoses of exclusion. This meant that the unclear constellation of symptoms didn't check the boxes for any specific condition, so a process of elimination was used. After many years of feeling uncertain about her health and questioning her medical team, she began looking for reasons not to trust them.

When she obtained second or third opinions from specialists, she sought out examples of their lack of knowledge or compassion. When others attempted to help her, she began to believe they were also part of a complicated matrix that intended to do her harm.

Ralph Waldo Emerson once said, "What we seek we shall find; what we flee from flees from us."

Mary found numerous examples of exactly what she was seeking. And unfortunately, many physicians ended up fleeing by discharging her from their practice.

The phenomenon of confirmation bias isn't exclusive to patients. Physicians and other healthcare providers also demonstrate this tendency.

John lived in a rural area and was experiencing symptoms of fatigue, swelling, and shortness of breath. Although he was elderly, he was in excellent physical shape. This resulted in his physicians dismissing his symptoms and ignoring his lab evidence of anemia. When I encouraged him to get a second opinion at an academic hospital two hours away, the physician found a bacterial infection on his heart valves that required immediate open-heart surgery.

The initial physician exhibited confirmation bias by failing to seek contradictory evidence to the assumption that his symptoms were mild and not indicative of a larger problem. The second physician kept an open mind on the diagnosis and avoided the tendency to dismiss any of the symptoms or labs as insignificant.

Confirmation bias can also show up between and among physicians. If an individual's medical chart suggests that the symptoms are psychosomatic, or *in their head*, a second physician reading this in advance of seeing the patient for the first time may look for examples to similarly dismiss the patient's reported experience.

In the last several years, there has been an increasing amount of attention given to the opioid epidemic, or overuse of narcotic pain relievers. For many patients, this starts as a limited-supply prescription for a painful procedure, such as wisdom tooth removal. It can then easily escalate to dependency and addiction.

I have personally seen many examples of healthcare professionals believing a patient is a drug-seeking addict upon request of a medication option for their pain. In many cases, this pain is legitimate and debilitating, such as pain associated with cancer. However, due to the extreme attention given to the opioid crisis and the scrutiny physicians find themselves under for prescribing these medications, judgments and biases are real and rampant.

Oftentimes, I encounter clients who were prescribed a medication that is known to be abused by the medical community. They were not counseled on the medication or given a warning on its abuse potential by the prescribing physician. Whether or not they become dependent on it, future physicians who see the medication on their list often make assumptions about the patient, their potential drug-seeking behavior, and their likelihood to be a "problem patient."

These beliefs, and the resulting labels, are both a challenge and significant obstacle to receiving optimal care.

Beliefs About Our Health

Personal beliefs about the cause of a specific health condition can influence the type of treatment a person seeks. If we believe our genetic predisposition is to blame for our health, we may feel helpless, hopeless, and a victim of our circumstances. We may even harbor anger or resentment for our parents as they passed down the genetic coding that ultimately caused our illness.

On the other hand, if we believe our lifestyle choices contributed to our condition, our approach may be entirely different. We may acknowledge that our family's medical history may have played a role, but the focus is on our choices and habits rather than our ancestry. This allows us to avoid the victim role and instead identify areas in our life that are in our control to change. Whether we begin to consume healthier food, limit our environmental toxins, increase our activity level, or otherwise, we move from passive surrender to active empowerment.

This area was studied extensively by Dr. Kelly Turner. As part of her

PhD from the University of California at Berkeley, she chose to focus her dissertation research on cases of radical remission. A radical remission (RR) is a cancer remission that occurs either without conventional medical treatment, after conventional treatment has failed to work, or when conventional and complementary methods are used in conjunction to overcome a dire prognosis.

In short, Dr. Turner wanted to know why RR survivors were alive and well without evidence of disease, despite being told by their physicians they would die in a short amount of time. Their physicians believed in a poor prognosis, while the patients did not.

And since these cases were considered anomalies, or anecdotes, to the medical field, they were not published in mainstream medical journals. In other words, one case example of a patient experiencing a spontaneous remission was not sufficient evidence to alert medical peers or the public that this could be possible for more patients.

After studying over fifteen hundred RR cases in over ten different countries, Dr. Turner published her findings in the books *Radical Remission* and *Radical Hope*. She identified ten separate healing factors that were used by all RR survivors to help heal their cancer. As you read over the list of healing factors, you may be surprised by how many relate to belief as well as emotional and spiritual factors.

The ten healing factors, in no particular order, are:

1. Engaging in exercise
2. Possessing a spiritual connection
3. Empowering yourself
4. Increasing positive emotions
5. Following your intuition
6. Releasing suppressed emotions
7. Changing your diet
8. Using herbs and supplements
9. Having strong reasons for living
10. Increasing social support

While the word *belief* is not listed, it's inherent in many of these factors. If you believe your genetics are a curse and the sole cause of your illness, you're less likely to make changes to your diet or increase your movement and exercise. If you believe your physician has all the answers and the prognosis is accurate, you're not likely to work on connecting to and following your intuition. And the more belief you place in another person's opinion or evaluation over your own, the less empowered you will feel and be.

On our podcast interview, Chris Wark stated, "Practically, it all starts with believing you can get well. Every person I know who has healed, including myself, believed they could get well. If the doctor said, 'You're dying,' they refused to believe it. They rejected that prognosis. In my circle, it's called a *medical hex* or a *curse*. It's incredible, the power of belief. And when somebody internalizes the fact that they will die in three months, they usually do. Like clockwork. If a patient believes they can get well, from there they take responsibility, and they start changing their life. One thing at a time."

How to Navigate Beliefs Within the Healthcare System

Now that we've established some ways in which our beliefs impact our healthcare experience, what should we do about it?

Our natural tendency can often involve both offensive and defensive behaviors. The beliefs and biases of our healthcare team can feel unfair and appear as the perfect cause for attack. On the flip side, we may have a hard time acknowledging our own belief systems and jump into defensive behavior when they're called out.

In Chapter 1, I outlined the nuances of the healthcare system and ways we can begin to accept some of these realities as they currently exist. In a similar way, I encourage my clients to acknowledge and ultimately accept that beliefs and biases are present. Spending our time and energy wishing this wasn't the case only results in our own suffering. Again, this doesn't mean we agree. It simply means we are making peace with what already is.

It is impossible to fully understand the underlying belief systems held by each of our medical team members. However, simply realizing that their opinions and decisions are informed by their beliefs will provide a lens through which you can make your own decisions about your care.

The beliefs you hold to be true can, and arguably should, be processed and navigated. First, reflect on your beliefs. Attempt to identify what you believe about your health, the medical system, and your ability to heal. Take some time to understand where each belief originated and what continues to influence them.

Second, gather credible information, not opinions. If you identify a belief that genetics were fully responsible for your diagnoses, seek trustworthy sources to confirm or deny this. Be open-minded and critically evaluate the information you find. Consider both your beliefs and the best available evidence.

Lastly, consider different perspectives. If a friend or family member seems to never get sick or need medical attention, try to understand how their belief systems may be playing a role. Maybe they believe their body has an innate ability to heal or they have made active and empowered changes to their lifestyle or environment. This is exactly why Dr. Turner chose to study RR survivors. She wanted to know why their approach seemed to produce health results that were in clear opposition to the beliefs of their physicians.

Navigating beliefs about health is a personal and ongoing journey. It's important to be flexible and open to new information, as our beliefs and understanding about health can evolve over time.

Peace Points

- Our beliefs about our health impact not only our choices, but the outcomes we experience.

- The beliefs of our medical team can also influence their treatment approach and our response.

- We can begin to question our beliefs once we identify them and consider different perspectives.

CHAPTER 4

IDENTITY

We take on various roles and identities throughout our lives. Illness identity, which arises from labels placed on us by the healthcare system, is a significant part of that.

I AM.

If you were to complete that sentence, how would it read? For many, it would sound something like "I am a daughter, wife, and mother to my two children." It might also include career specifics or other titles and roles.

For someone facing illness, it may sound like "I am sick" or "I am a cancer patient" or simply "I am tired." For my dad, I heard and watched his confidence shake as soon as he was told, "You have cancer." He no longer saw himself as a whole being, but rather parts with and parts without cancer. It was almost as if he owned a diagnosis like owning a piece of real estate in disrepair that he couldn't sell or walk away from.

We rarely, if ever, question who we really are. Michael Singer, author of the New York Times number one bestseller *The Untethered Soul*, encourages us to question this deeply and often. If you are a mother to two children, does that mean you were someone different before you gave birth?

If you are a cancer patient now, who were you before the diagnosis?

These questions help us analyze the language we use and ultimately the identities we are holding for ourselves.

Identifiers in the Healthcare System

The healthcare system works largely on labels, titles, and identities. Staff members wear badges with large letters to show their credentials. Patients in a hospital wear a wristband, and their visitors wear a white sticker on their chest indicating such.

When referring to patients, the medical team uses terminology like "the liver cancer patient in Room 2023" or "the patient with cystic fibrosis in Room 3500." The front page of a patient's medical chart usually includes a long list of every diagnosis made up to the present time, ultimately providing an endless stream of labeling.

Additional identifiers include medical record numbers, billing account numbers, and biometric information for facilities utilizing more advanced technology.

Without question, many of these identifiers are essential to accurate patient identification and safe healthcare delivery. Proper use of patient identifiers can help protect privacy, prevent unauthorized access to sensitive information, and help ensure the right patient receives the right treatment.

Also, without question, stigmatization is a real phenomenon within healthcare that can affect a patient's personal and social life.

I interviewed Caroline on my podcast a few years ago. She had been diagnosed with four meningioma brain tumors and explained how this diagnosis took over every moment of her day. She found it difficult to be present. She looked at her children and couldn't help but wonder if she would be around to watch them grow up.

Caroline so deeply identified with her tumors that she named them—Regina, Sheila, Melissa, and Walter.

"When we start to identify with our diagnosis, that's ultimately a symptom of the grief we are experiencing because of our diagnosis," she explained. When she opened up about her grief, which included friendships and life goals lost, she started to realize that she didn't know anything about who she was. She only knew she had four brain tumors.

Her *I am* statement may have sounded like "I am a meningioma patient with four brain tumors." But is that who she really is? Did her true identity change the minute she received the diagnosis?

The process of identification can also be fueled by bias within the medical system.

Clara came to me frustrated that she had been prescribed a muscle relaxant named Soma, but her new physician was unwilling to refill it. She also voiced concern over what appeared to be judgment at the pharmacy when she would pick up her medication.

What Clara didn't know about this medication, and the resultant identifiers of her as a patient taking it, were absolutely hurting her.

Soma, also known by its generic name carisoprodol, gets metabolized in the body to meprobamate, which is known as a tranquilizer or anxiolytic. Due to this, it is labeled as a controlled substance with a potential for abuse. It is commonplace for a healthcare professional to see this medication on a patient's list and make assumptions about their potential addictive behaviors.

Clara, who never asked for Soma and didn't fully understand what it was or how it worked in the body, was being labeled as an addict who was abusing the medication. To her, it was nothing more than another prescription that she was taking per the doctor's instructions. To the physicians, nurses, and pharmacists taking care of her, the judgments had been made and would be difficult to undo.

The medical system also tends to focus on the deficits or problems that may arise from a diagnosis rather than a patient's strengths or abilities. If an infant is found to have a congenital condition, the parents are often told what their child will likely never be able to do as a result. When a patient is diagnosed with a progressive condition, such as multiple sclerosis (MS), the conversation is typically focused on the likelihood and timeline of losing the ability to walk.

A patient can identify as an otherwise healthy and able adult one day, and the next identify as an MS patient who will soon be in a wheelchair. This shift in identity can, and does, change a person's life trajectory.

Illness Identity

Once the medical system has added its labels, patients then find their minds begin to run wild with storylines that fit this new character.

Previously healthy thirty-year-old now sick with lupus and unable to do the things she loves. A patient with this narrative might decline invitations to outings because she believes she is too sick. She may be self-conscious about any external confirmation of her diagnosis, such as a rash, which can affect her confidence. In turn, she may avoid applying for jobs that are client-facing, which she would have excelled at in the past.

Active grandfather of five now disabled from the progressive nature of Parkinson's disease. This storyline may cause him to avoid activities with his grandchildren, even when he is still able. He may focus on people he knows or celebrities who have suffered from Parkinson's and assume his course will be the same or worse. He may cancel upcoming trips or completely alter his retirement plan because of this diagnosis.

The environment patients find themselves in can have a significant impact on their self-identity. Patty was a middle-aged female who was previously high-functioning in her job. When I met her, she was suffering from surgical complications that resulted in her living in a long-term care facility. She was surrounded by patients several decades older who shared very little, if any, common interests with her. They were visited by their adult children, while she was visited by her coworkers and elderly parents. Over time, patients in this situation can find themselves beginning to identify with those around them rather than who they were just four weeks prior.

This phenomenon is more than hyperbole. Medical literature defines illness identity as the degree to which a chronic health condition, such as heart disease, is integrated into someone's identity (Van Bulck 2018).[9] The degree to which patients define themselves in terms of their disease is further divided into four constructs: *engulfment, rejection, acceptance,* and *enrichment.*

Engulfment indicates that a patient's disease completely defines and dominates that person's identity. Rejection and acceptance are as the titles suggest—specifically rejecting the incorporation of diagnosis into self-identity and accepting the identification with disease without being overwhelmed by it. Enrichment is the state in which patients feel their diagnosis has changed their perspective on life and allowed for personal development.

Researchers not only developed standardized questionnaires to evaluate these illness identity states, but they have studied how these constructs impact symptomatology.

As one might anticipate, patients who fell into the acceptance category had fewer depression and anxiety symptoms. Engulfment, on the other hand, resulted in higher perceptions of depression and anxiety. Both engulfment and rejection were associated with having more physical symptoms of disease.

Interestingly, enrichment was also associated with more significant disease symptomatology, possibly due to this being a prerequisite to personal growth from the impact of disease.

So how do we face a diagnosis with acceptance of what the medical system believes, while avoiding becoming engulfed or dominated by it?

Identity Beyond Illness

The healthcare system is ill-equipped, and the staff is largely untrained, to help patients deal with these identity issues as they arise. Many

9   Van Bulck et al., "Illness Identity," 4.

physicians and other providers also lack the self-awareness to realize any biases they may have and how this may impact the way they interact with their patients.

We are largely left to do our own inner work as we navigate and ultimately choose how a new diagnosis affects our self-identity.

Lyn, one of my friends who deeply knew her identity beyond her illness, said it best. "I am so much bigger than cancer. I am a whole being. And I have achieved incredible things in my life. I am capable of incredible things. And I feel like she [her physician] doesn't know that. It's just about the cancer and how it's going to kill you. And I just want to say no. The story continues. There's more."

Lyn knew who she was. She was more than cancer. More than any label the healthcare system placed on her chart. More than her physician could possibly know in the short timeframe she had worked with her.

She knew her story would continue. And it has, even beyond her passing.

What Lyn realized without knowing it is that the biomedical model is lacking in its ability to understand the whole person. Patients are indeed bigger and much more complex than their biology and list of diagnoses.

Start to see the diagnosis as an opinion, which it is. In effect, a medical professional has provided you with an opinion, and that opinion happens to come with a title. It is not a physical birthmark that you are unable to remove. It's simply an expert narrative that may not be accurate and may be able to be reversed if it is indeed accurate.

I encourage you to reflect back on the statement we began this chapter with.

I am.

How does that sentence continue? What is your true essence? Who are you without the attached medical narrative?

This work requires you to dive deep. Deeper than you may have ever gone. I have included a guided meditation at the end of this chapter to help you with this important work.

You are a whole being. *You* have achieved incredible things, and you're capable of incredible things. *Your* story continues.

Guided Meditation

Settle into a comfortable space and position. Allow your eyes to close or gently gaze downward. Connect to the present moment as if you are meeting with a longtime friend you haven't seen in a while. Notice the sensation of the surface beneath you. Feel the temperature of the room you are in. Hear the sounds around you, both in your immediate environment and farther in the distance.

Allow your breath to be your anchor. Notice its natural rhythm and cadence. Follow an entire breath from the inhale, down to your lungs, and back up to exhale. Continue this for three more breaths. Connect in appreciation for your life breath.

Imagine looking in a mirror in front of you. You are wearing many layers of clothing, similar to what you might wear in a very cold environment. Beyond your base layers, you have a fleece shirt, light jacket, and heavier jacket. You also have a thick scarf around your neck and a knitted beanie cap on your head. Mittens cover your hands, and you are wearing heavy snow boots on your feet.

Imagine each one of these layers represents a title or identity you are holding. Notice the weight of these layers and how they place a burden on your body to carry. Feel the heaviness against your skin.

Now, imagine watching yourself in the mirror remove each of these layers. First, remove the snow boots and the associated title they represent. This may be *parent*. Or *daughter*. Or something different.

Next, free your hands of the mittens and watch them, and that title, symbolically fall to the floor as well. This may be your job title. Or volunteer position. Or something else.

Slowly begin to do the same with each subsequent layer. Say out loud, or quietly in your mind, what each layer represents. Include any medical diagnoses you may have been given by the healthcare system. Allow them all to fall to the floor.

Notice the shift in burden felt by your body. This may include the physical weight lifted from removing the layers. It may also include the mental and emotional weight each of those titles represent.

Once the layers are all removed, look at yourself in the mirror and ask: Who *am* I? Who am I without those layers? Without those titles? Who is this person looking back at me? Even deeper, who is the consciousness witnessing the person in the mirror?

Sit in this space for a few more minutes. Reconnect to your breath if you need to. Allow any and all emotions and insights to surface without judgment or a need to change them. Simply notice.

When you're ready, reconnect to the space you are in. The surface beneath you. The air around you. The sounds.

And slowly begin to open your eyes.

This would be a good time to journal any insights that arose for you during this meditation.

Peace Points

- Our self-identities are largely influenced by the healthcare system and its labels.
- We can learn a lot from others who have experienced illness identity.
- We can also work on releasing the impact of these identities through deep inner work, including meditation.

CHAPTER 5

UNLEARNING

With several decades of life experience, we have learned much about the world. This includes roles, relationships, and societal norms. While some of the dots we have connected are serving us, many are not. Unlearning belief systems surrounding the healthcare system and how we interact with it can ultimately save our lives.

Why Unlearn?

FROM the day of birth, learning begins.

First, our life "school" teaches us about sleep/wake cycles, how to get the nourishment we need, and how our bodies work. We then start learning our native language, which allows us to communicate our needs and wants verbally. Along the way, our experiences begin to weave themselves into the fabric of our life quilt, and connections begin to appear between dots that previously existed in isolation.

Until we are able to navigate this planet independently, opinions, stories, and generational truths are passed down to us at home, in school, in church, and in other impressionable settings. By an early age, many of us have begun to believe Jesus is a middle-aged light-skinned male with medium-length brown hair, and that good grades equate with a higher potential for success. We have also been taught to be respectful, "good" kids who don't talk back or question the often-heard parental response, "Because I said so."

As such, it's not too much of a stretch of the imagination to extrapolate how the healthcare dots become connected for us early in life. Depending on our parents' values and beliefs, many of us grow up confident that doctors hold some symbolic "key" to the answers of why the body becomes ill. And just as we were taught not to question our parents' authority, we similarly should never be so disrespectful as to question the key holder of the healthcare knowledge. We watch our parents bring us to the doctor, explain what we have been experiencing, and walk away with a paper that contains the answer to make it go away.

So many dots connected in so few years. Good grades result in . . . success. Good kids . . . don't talk back. Good patients . . . don't ask questions.

For many generations, the accepted etiquette in an exam room was to sit quietly, speak only when spoken to, and follow all instructions provided. In fact, medical compliance was such a core belief that it earned an official definition in the late 1970s as "the extent to which the patient's behavior (in terms of taking medications, following diets, or executing other lifestyle changes) coincides with medical or health advice" (Trostle 1997).[10]

When I attended pharmacy school in the late 1990s and early 2000s, patient compliance was an emphasized topic woven throughout my training. We role-played cases in which we identified areas of noncompliance. We brainstormed strategies to help patients struggling with compliance become more—you guessed it—compliant. Since it was all discussed within the context of helping people, my bright-eyed, bushy-tailed colleagues and I eagerly allowed our elder professors to

---

10   Trostle, "The History and Meaning of Patient Compliance," 109.

impart their wisdom on us. We nodded our heads in agreement and voraciously wrote down all the ways we could tell our patients to take their medications as prescribed.

Good pharmacy students . . . help patients become more compliant.

The tide is turning, though, and millennials are leading that turn. This young generation is the most curious demographic in the United States, open to new possibilities, and are through accepting the status quo (Merck 2018).[11] Why is curiosity important? It helps us start to question truths that have been passed down for decades, even centuries in some cases. It allows us to look critically at ourselves, what we believe, and how those beliefs came to be. It opens the door to differentiate fact from opinion. Curiosity helps us wonder and ask *what if?*

What if there is an intersection between the physician's book knowledge and the patient's intuitive knowledge?

What if silent compliance hurts not only the patient who isn't permitted to ask questions, but also the physician who isn't allowed the opportunity to think outside the boundaries of traditional medical training as a recipient of patient-directed questions?

What if there is more value to unlearning and disconnecting from Google medical searches and instead connecting with our inner wisdom and guidance?

Although there are clear generational influences and imprints on our beliefs and value systems, society plays a significant role as well. We look to the news and media to tell us what is societally acceptable. The COVID-19 pandemic put an unprecedented spotlight on this. As a planet, we collectively watched our leaders turn an abundance of uncertainty into directives that had extreme societal implications.

Mask mandates turned into a whole new set of connected dots. In some circles, wearing a mask meant . . . *caring citizen.* In other circles, wearing a mask indicated . . . *subservient follower.* Vaccine mandates took societal pressures to a heightened level, placing some workers at risk of

---

11   Merck, "State of Curiosity Report," 9.

losing their jobs. In some communities, an individual's choice not to be vaccinated resulted in isolation and separation from friends and family.

We were asked to connect a seemingly endless number of dots around an illness that remained largely misunderstood. On the other hand, we have clear examples in the history of our nation and world that suggest some dots, in hindsight, deserve connecting and reconnecting (e.g., vaccine-eradication of infectious diseases like polio and measles).

It is only now, years after the first COVID-19 case appeared, that we are doing the important work of unlearning and disconnecting. What appeared to be a permanent shift to remote work is now being reevaluated. The effectiveness and adaptability of present public health measures are being questioned. And the economic predictability of certain industries requires a deeper understanding.

Some of my most valuable lessons have come from an openness to *un*learn. This was extremely difficult for me, a self-identified Type A personality who prided herself on learning all the things and earning stellar grades to prove it. I wasn't the kid who asked a lot of questions. I observed, listened, and followed the lead of my parents and teachers. Tell me to study chapters ten through twelve in any given textbook, and you could be sure I would have most, if not all, of the content within those chapters memorized. I never questioned the material or even wondered who the originating source was. It was simply information I was instructed to learn—so I did.

When my father died, I became the most curious I had ever been. I asked questions I would never have dreamed of asking prior to his death. I watched my father become a physician's dream—a compliant patient. He kept meticulous records of all the instructions he received. If he was told to take a medication four times a day, you could trust he would spread the dosing interval out to exactly every six hours and not miss a single dose. He never missed an appointment and always arrived at least thirty minutes early.

The only question he asked was when his body would be ready to return to work. When his last oncologist said that there was "nothing more to be done," I remember wondering how that could be. How could my father, the stellar compliant patient who did everything right, be receiving this news?

The *what ifs* slowly began to form in my mind.

What if his dedicated unquestioning compliance is part of the problem?

What if the physician doesn't and simply can't be expected to know everything?

What if there is a better way to use the physician's knowledge as more of a consultant than a dictator?

What if there are other treatment approaches that could augment, supplement, or even replace what had been prescribed by his Western-trained, conventional doctor?

Unfortunately, by the time I became curious and started questioning Western medicine, it was too late for my dad. That fact didn't stop me; it fueled me!

I may not have been able to extend his life, but I was certainly on a mission to unlearn everything that so clearly wasn't working in the modern healthcare system and begin to learn the expansive world that exists beyond it.

After over a decade and a half of working inside the system, then trusting that same system to help my dad, it was a hard pill to swallow to finally realize that our healthcare system doesn't have all the answers. Medications aren't the answer to all medical symptoms. Food does indeed matter and can't possibly be acknowledged in a system that doesn't train its physicians to understand this. While Western medicine plays an undeniably vital role in many situations, such as emergent surgery, there's a vast gray area that it simply isn't equipped to address. This merger of black and white space includes near-death experiences, spontaneous remissions, and meditation-directed healing, to name a few.

As I reflect on my dad's conventional cancer care, I realize that not one person asked him what he ate during the day. None of his providers asked him how he was doing mentally or emotionally. No one seemed to be interested in factors I now know play a significant role in healing. When he would lose weight, the advice was always to consume more calories. If that meant ice cream three times a day, so be it. Despite the abundance of intake forms and triage visits with nurses, not one health-care provider or staff member asked my dad how he was handling his diagnosis. No one thought it would be helpful to know if the prognosis he received or the side effects from the chemotherapy were causing him anxiety or depression.

The dot connected for me during pharmacy school, namely that Western medicine holds all the answers, quickly faded and instead became: Western medicine is far from perfect.

When I began to analyze some of these dots and allow the process of unlearning to take place, my curiosity allowed space for unchartered growth. Rather than accept the status quo as a sad, but true reality of the healthcare system that had no answer or resolution, I decided that the more effective approach was to question.

If Western medicine actually doesn't have all the answers, where else might I look?

If the traditional healthcare system isn't equipped to educate patients on the healing effects of proper nutrition, who is able to fill in this gap?

If physicians don't have the time, compassion, or both to evaluate the mental and emotional impacts of illness and its treatments, how else would one fill these significant needs?

I almost felt like I was making up for lost time from my curiosity-lacking childhood.

Let's Begin Unlearning

I hope I have opened the door for you to start your own process of unlearning. Each of us will find ourselves facing a different set of belief systems and existing paradigms. Some of these have served us well in the past but may no longer be serving us in our current season of life.

Others have never proven to be helpful, yet we continue to hold on to them for a variety of reasons.

One common pattern I see in my work with clients is choosing familiarity over uncertainty, even when that which is familiar negatively impacts our lives. We know how to sit quietly in an exam room, but speaking up hasn't been modeled for us, so we lack the confidence to do so.

Another is often both cultural and generational and involves the concept of respect. When we are taught to respect authority at all costs, including our parents, teachers, and physicians, we often indirectly dilute the ability to respect ourselves. This can lead to an inability or unwillingness to listen to the gentle whispers and nudges we receive from our intuition or "gut." We know the headaches we have been experiencing may be a side effect from a recently prescribed medication, but we want to be "good" patients and take what the doctor ordered.

The good news is that we can do hard things, including unlearning the belief systems that aren't serving us and relearning how to live a more curious and authentic life that supports our well-being. In the remainder of this chapter, I will cover a few common belief systems that beg us to begin questioning.

I would also encourage you to spend some time identifying additional truths you may be holding that have quieted both your internal and external voice. The guided meditation at the end of this chapter can help with this process. Regarding your health and healthcare, the following "truths" are—to be honest—worth questioning.

Patient Versus Expert

The term *patient* is defined as a person receiving, or registered to receive, medical treatment. It is how we are identified in the healthcare system. Hospital and clinic settings teach us how these roles play out. The medical staff wear badges clearly showing their titles as NURSE or PHYSICIAN in large, bolded, capitalized letters. They walk with a quickness in their step and an appearance of confidence.

Patients are those who don't wear a badge. They sit quietly in the waiting room, either reading a tattered magazine or staring at their phones to stay distracted. They are there to listen, answer a few pointed questions, and ultimately be given instructions they are expected to follow. They walk slowly, and visibly show their understanding of their place in the hierarchy.

But *what if* you unlearn the parts of this script that aren't serving you? *What if*, instead of seeing yourself as a patient, you began to see yourself as a *subject matter expert*? Much like you respect the extreme amount of training and knowledge gained by your physician, you also start respecting the fact that you are the only one who has lived in your body since birth. As such, there truly is no better-trained expert on what it's like to be you.

And to reassure you that this is not simply my opinion, allow the US Department of Energy's definition of subject matter expert to convince you: "An individual who by education or training, and/or experience, is a recognized expert on a particular subject, topic, or system."

You may not have a healthcare education, but you undoubtedly have the experience of living in your own body. *You are an expert on you!*

It may not yet be recognized widely in a system that gives preference to knowledge gained through education and training, but not even the most highly regarded medical professional can or will ever know you better than you know yourself.

As you work to unlearn the societal role of patient and learn the role of expert, how might this impact the way you show up to your medical appointments?

Maybe you no longer passively wait to be called by the intake nurse while reading a magazine. Instead, you may opt to review the notes you wrote about the timeline of symptoms you have been experiencing over the last few weeks.

Maybe you no longer stare at a social media app on your phone in an attempt to distract yourself, but rather mentally prepare for the questions you want to ask and additional questions you may generate based on the visit.

This doesn't mean that shifting the perception of your role has to equate to downplaying the role of the physician. Lifting yourself as the patient doesn't have to result in lowering the physician. It is indeed true that your physician has undergone a level of training more rigorous and lengthy than most people could comprehend. I also believe it is largely true that physicians do so with honest and good intentions to help those in their care.

It is, however, also true that your experiential knowledge of your body is an extremely important part of the equation that helps you heal.

While the healthcare system may never pivot to calling patients "experts," you can start calling yourself an expert. Today.

And I encourage you to do so.

Consultant Versus Dictator

It's understandably difficult to read and respond to a person with whom you are in a relationship when you aren't clear on the roles of the relationship. We learn to connect several dots at a young age regarding relationships. Parents . . . hold expectations of respect and obedience. Later in life, we expand this concept beyond our parental boundaries. Friends . . . offer a source of support throughout your life.

Without conscious awareness, many also begin to define relationships with their doctors. Physicians . . . dictate your healthcare, being superior in knowledge.

In each of the above situations, once these dots are connected and you accept your role in the relationship, you fall into character much like an actor on a stage.

But *what if*?

What if these roles can be redefined? *What if* there's a healthier, more productive relationship you can have with your doctor, and doing so requires you to reframe the rules of the relationship?

What if instead of dictator and passive follower, the characters were consultant and consultee? As a consultee, you identify a medical concern for which you would like a knowledgeable consultant. You hire a physician to offer advice during a set consultation time. You ask the questions you want answered, express your gratitude for the consult, and ultimately decide what your next step should be. It may be following your consultant's treatment plan. It might be taking time to meditate, pray, or simply allow yourself space to align with the decision that feels best. It might be seeking a second consultant.

The point here is there is no legal, ethical, or otherwise named requirement for you to follow any individual physician's plan. If you decide the proposed plan isn't right for you, you will not face legal recourse. Your ethics will not be in question and no notice will be sent by your physician to all other physicians indicating you are a poor follower. You simply move on as a consultee, and your consultant will do the same.

Unlearning and relearning the roles of this relationship could literally save your life.

Fact Versus Opinion

We all understand the word *opinion* to be an estimation, a view, or a judgment.

An opinion might be based on a body of knowledge, but that's certainly not a prerequisite. It has become commonplace for us to reference seeing another specialist as "getting a second opinion." And that's precisely what we are doing, specifically taking what was told to us by physician number one, bringing the same data to physician number two, and determining if we receive the same output. If the output is different, we then have to decide if we want a third opinion or if we feel opinion number one or number two is more correct than the other.

There is an interesting gap in this process that undoubtedly affects our decision-making. We have not been taught to label the diagnosis, prognosis, and treatment plan by physician number one as an "opinion." In other words, people don't commonly refer to this as the "first opinion";

rather, it becomes the standard against which others are compared.

Your decision to obtain a second opinion is usually based on your not liking or agreeing with what you were initially told. If you are in agreement with physician number one, you may likely consider the information to be factual, and you proceed as instructed. If you are not in agreement, you may seek a second opinion.

What if we realize that they were all opinions?

The first physician combined knowledge, training, experience, and perspective into a professional opinion on what is happening, why it might be happening, and what should happen next. There was likely a strong factual component to this opinion, but it ultimately was and will always be an opinion. Much like the second and possibly third opinion, it's all an estimation subject to human error and biases.

When we realize this, we can open the door to unlearning the belief that every individual assessment or advice is factual. The term *differential diagnosis* exists for a good reason. When lab results and symptoms could possibly be matched to several diagnoses, physicians create a list of possibilities. Sometimes they discuss this list with colleagues to gather their opinions. Other times, they simply choose the most likely answer from that list based on the patient's objective and subjective data as well as statistical probability. That choice can be, and often is, incorrect. It is an *opinion*—based on a wide body of knowledge.

However, as we know, the human body is complex, and our understanding of it continues to have large gaps. As such, what if you treated *all* medical advice as opinion? That doesn't mean you disregard it or override it with the opinions you read on Google. It's simply a mindset shift.

Opinions are subject to change, can be incorrect, and should be viewed similar to a hired consultant giving you their best guess. What you as the receiver of that information do with it is ultimately in your hands.

And that, my friends, is a fact.

Peace Points

- Become curious about your healthcare journey.

- Open your mind to unlearn belief systems that are no longer serving you.

- Consider your role as an expert on your own health and as a consultee seeking a consultant's advice, which ultimately is one of many possible opinions.

Guided Meditation

Find an area of your home or office that is comfortable and mostly free from distractions. You may either sit upright or lie down, respecting your body's preference in this moment. Close your eyes softly, or gently gaze downward if that feels better.

Before we begin the practice, remember that meditation is not about perfecting anything. It's simply about being aware, connecting to your body, and noticing what emotions or intuitive messages may arise. If you're new to this practice, fantastic and welcome. If you've been meditating for a while, feel free to adjust this practice to best fit your needs.

First, let's connect to our breath. It's common for us to feel disconnected from our breath and not notice when we are holding our breath or breathing shallowly. In this moment, we will simply take notice, without judgment. As you inhale and exhale naturally, how does it feel? Shallow? Deep? Fast? Slow? The breath is a helpful anchor to return to if and when your thoughts appear.

In this chapter, we have explored the concept of unlearning. To help you dive deeper into this concept, I want you to imagine a white board in front of you. On that white board, imagine taking a marker and separating the board into two vertical columns. In your mind, label the left column "KNOWING" in all caps and the right column "knowing" in all lowercase letters.

Now, allow your mind to fill the left-hand column of KNOWING with facts or beliefs you hold to be true because someone taught them to you. This could be from parents, teachers, coaches, or mentors. These facts or beliefs could be related to relationships, religion, academics, or similar topics. Take a few minutes here to explore what comes to mind.

Next, imagine filling the right-hand column of knowing with facts or beliefs you hold to be true only because of a deeper understanding. You hold these truths not because someone taught them to you. You may not even be able to explain why you know them to be true. You simply do. And no person on the planet could convince you otherwise. Take a few minutes to explore what comes to mind for this column.

Now take a step back from this imaginary whiteboard. Review your two columns. Take note if one column was easier to fill than the other. Reflect on what came up for you during this process. Maybe even choose one or two items from the first column to look at with deeper curiosity. Do you still believe these to be true after your review? Why or why not?

Return, just for a minute, to your breath. Reanchor here, both to your body and to the present moment. Send yourself gratitude for taking this time of self-exploration and reflection. When you're ready, open your eyes and, if you'd like, take out a journal and write down any insights from this practice.

CHAPTER 6

COMMUNICATION

The medical system trains its physicians to communicate in the fewest words possible to express their knowledge and understanding of what a patient is facing. Patients, on the other hand, are seeking a deeper relationship that allows them to feel seen and heard. This extreme difference in communication styles can feel unsurmountable but can be navigated peacefully with a few shifts in approach.

GEORGE Bernard Shaw once said, "The single biggest problem in communication is the illusion that it has taken place."

While he wasn't specifically referring to the medical system when he spoke those words, their applicability is quite striking.

My dad's level of communication with his medical team was reflective of his unwavering belief in their knowledge and ability to save his life. They spoke; he nodded his head in agreement. They gave him prescriptions and instructions; he followed them. I, on the other hand, wanted and needed to know *why, what,* and *how*. Specifically, when his oncologist outlined the treatment plan, I asked why that plan was chosen and what the medical literature reported on its effectiveness and safety. When the physician referenced possible side effects and treating them as they might arise, I asked how my dad would know he was experiencing them and how the physician planned on addressing them.

I rarely nodded my head without sufficient follow-up information.

It's not likely shocking to hear that many patients feel dismissed and unheard in their communication with physicians. This is a result of many factors, including the limited time given to them during appointments, the focus on technology and charting over direct eye-to-eye contact, and the complicated medical language being spoken.

I often describe the "gray space" when describing my role as a patient advocate. This is the invisible yet palpable space I believe lies between the patient and the physician. The space that often feels difficult to access, almost as if it is walled off with impenetrable borders. It's in that space where I do my best work in bringing together the messages from both the patient and the physician. In this space, I help all parties feel heard and understood.

Achieving success in the gray space requires an in-depth understanding of how both sides communicate.

Physician Communication

Beginning in medical school and further modeled in residency, physicians are taught to limit their words. This may sound counterintuitive, as other highly regarded professionals in our modern society are often known to be verbose. Lawyers, for example, use many scholarly words to create arguments, rebut arguments, and ultimately win their point on behalf of their clients.

Physicians, on the other hand, are taught the opposite. While they are expected to know and fully understand the language of medicine, they are also asked to speak concisely and in absence of excess.

In fact, a buzzword often used during training is "high-yield."

This term refers to the material that will yield the greatest gain. During medical school, this is usually used in reference to that which students will most likely be tested on during exams. The opposite, of course, is "low-yield" and is assigned a lesser priority for study purposes. These terms continue to be used through residency training to ensure concise communication between residents and attending physicians.

When a resident is sharing physical exam findings and understanding of a patient's condition to the attending physician, there is an unstated agreement that only the most high-yield facts are shared. The attending is not interested in "fluff" or information that is not deemed relevant to the patient's medical case.

Due to this, resident physicians train to speak only when their words hold value in achieving the goal of diagnosing and treating their patients.

A significant driver for this high-yield culture is the overburdened status of the healthcare system and the limited time available to effectively care for the quantity of patients needing care. Another term, "protected time," is also used to highlight the need for time prioritization. Lengthy discussions with unnecessary words lead to longer days in the clinic and hospital, which in turn results in less protected time for physicians to conduct their other nonclinical duties and spend time with their families at home.

On a positive note, residents are usually strongly encouraged by their attending physicians to sit down with their patients and spend adequate time to establish rapport and obtain an accurate and thorough medical history. However, one can extrapolate and imagine that the high-yield communication style that slowly develops during a physician's medical training ends up also being used in interactions with patients. The time limitations within the healthcare system continue to fuel and require short, concise, pointed conversations that include only the information believed to be most important.

When presented with a patient who is talkative and does not reflect a similar attentiveness to high-yield facts, the physician often has a difficult time screening through the abundance of words to locate those that will help make a clinical judgment. Therefore, points that are important to the patient get missed, and the patient feels unheard or even dismissed.

In addition, the direct way in which physicians are trained to communicate often results in the delivery of patient diagnoses feeling cold and as though they are lacking compassion. While rarely reflective of an actual lack of empathy, this does highlight the need for physicians to disconnect even slightly from the emotions of their work. With countless new diagnoses to deliver to patients every day, the messengers almost have no choice but to distance themselves from the depth of emotions this would otherwise bring.

This lack of warmth and compassion can often be felt in emergency departments as the volume and severity of cases is typically higher than that of an outpatient clinic. My friend, Liz, drove herself to the ER with severe abdominal pain. Imaging was ordered of the affected area, and a pancreatic mass was found. Liz was a young, relatively new mother of two girls at the time and wasn't expecting anything more than gallbladder or appendix concerns that could relatively easily be resolved with possible surgery.

Instead, she was visited by the physician and told matter-of-factly, "Your tests show a mass in your pancreas. We will need further tests to determine next steps." Others in the medical field may argue that the words said were indeed true and without unnecessary fluff to confuse the message.

Most patients, on the other hand, are like Liz, who froze after the words *mass in your pancreas*. She immediately thought of her two daughters and the possibility she wouldn't be there to watch them grow up. All instructions that may have been communicated after those words were lost and unprocessed.

And thus begins the development of the gray area.

Patient Communication

With most patients not having been through medical training, the communication style of physicians described above is not well understood.

Patients simply want what most humans are seeking—time and attention to their concerns. Unfortunately, in traditional medical practices, time is a resource that is in both high demand and limited supply.

While physicians are being trained to focus on high-yield facts, patients are preparing to share as much information as possible during their appointments. They are journaling their symptoms multiple times per day, taking note of their food consumption, and logging blood pressure and blood sugar readings when necessary. In addition, they are completing the physician's lengthy intake forms with thorough and detailed answers.

To the general public, it seems reasonable that collecting and delivering the maximum amount of information would help the physician be sufficiently armed to make well-informed clinical decisions. And in a utopian world, as well as some concierge-style practices, this is perfectly reasonable and does indeed help the physician do just that.

In the traditional fee-for-service practice that allots fifteen to twenty minutes per office visit, however, it's simply not. The food and blood pressure logs may receive a quick glance from the physician. The intake forms that were so meticulously completed may never be read at all.

In addition, patients desire a humanistic relationship with their physician. They often share recent pictures of their kids or find an opportunity to expand on their excitement over a recent career change. In return, they hope to also learn more about the physician's family life and hobby interests. In essence, they have a desire to get back to the historical picture of the primary care practice—the kindly family doctor.

This interest in a deeper connection is at the core of who we are as humans.

Although this may be hard to believe for those whose experience has been contrary, many physicians also genuinely desire a similar depth in connection with their patients. They, too, understand that the patient-physician relationship is made stronger through effective communication, empathy, collaboration, and trust. They simply aren't given the time to nurture this part of the relationship in the current healthcare landscape.

A client of mine recently lost her husband to cancer at a young age. She lived alone and wanted to share this part of her story with her rheumatologist during their visit. After all, grief significantly impacts both the mind and body and was therefore relevant to her health at that time.

While the rheumatologist did acknowledge her grief and express his condolences, the figurative show had to go on. There was a waiting room full of patients, and he still had to review her labs and make medication adjustments accordingly.

She was able to observe the physician's demeanor and brevity in communication and quickly realized that elaborating on how the grief was affecting her was not being welcomed. Had he spent an additional five to ten minutes allowing her to open up about her emotional response, he may have been able to validate the degree to which the stress was exacerbating her condition. Maybe that would have led him to maintain the same medications while encouraging her to work with a therapist on processing her grief.

Maybe the act of simply listening actively would have provided her with the emotional connection she needed at that time. And maybe the physician wished he had time to provide her with that support. However, the end result was the patient not feeling support and the physician not given the resources to feel he could provide it.

Barriers to Communication

I would be remiss to not address the multitude of communication barriers that make this gray space more difficult to access.

In the US, English is not the primary language for many patients. Our culture is a melting pot of many backgrounds, and therefore, language barriers can present a challenge for the patient-physician relationship. While most healthcare systems have translating services, the effective communication of symptoms and concerns from the patient and medical instructions from the physician are often negatively impacted.

In addition to differences in language, cultural differences can present as a barrier to communication. Certain health issues, such as mental health or sexual concerns, may be considered taboo in some cultures. As a result, these issues may go unaddressed.

Cultural differences may also play into power dynamics. In many cultures, the physician is seen as the expert and authority who is not to be questioned. This can leave the patient feeling intimidated or uncomfortable asking questions or seeking clarification.

As mentioned before, health literacy can be a significant barrier to the patient-physician relationship. Even if both the physician and patient speak English as their primary language, medical jargon can leave many patients feeling as if they have been dropped involuntarily in another country.

Healthcare professionals not only take a medical terminology class in college, but they are exposed to and trained in this for many years. It's not surprising that a patient lacking this training and experience would feel lost and incapable of meeting the physician in the gray space.

The Gray Space

So, how do we bring these two communication styles and needs together? How do we bridge the divide and break down the barriers in the gray space?

We must first understand where each party is coming from and where they are headed.

As we discussed, physicians are coming from a fast-paced training and working environment where time is limited. They are expected to identify and fix complicated problems in less time than it takes most of us to finish our morning cup of coffee.

Patients are coming from their home environments that may feel isolating or full of worry about the future. They are uncertain about their upcoming medical journey, and they desperately want their physician to care about them as more than another medical record number. Consumed by their diagnosis and trying to figure out what it means, their sympathetic nervous system is in chronic overdrive.

How do we meet in the middle?

I believe it's important to let your physician know what is and is not working during your visits. After all, none of us can change that of which we aren't aware. Would you prefer that your physician sits rather than stands? Does the doctor's attention to the computer screen make you feel unattended to? Would you like a more detailed explanation of either your diagnosis or the treatment plan?

Your physician deserves a fighting chance to provide you with what you need.

Beyond communicating your needs and expectations to your physician, focus on what *is* in your control—how you navigate your own healthcare journey.

Knowing that physicians have a limited amount of time, we can meet them where they are rather than become frustrated at the realities of the healthcare system. Understanding that their training has molded them into speaking concisely and without unnecessary emotion can help us avoid making assumptions about their level of care and compassion.

This may mean coming prepared to a visit to discuss only one primary concern. If we feel that concern is largely impacted by a recent personal event, bringing that up along with its relevance to the concern is justifiable and appropriate.

In my work with clients, I offer a template that can be used to prepare to discuss the highest-priority topics during the visit. Are you most concerned with a recent rash that developed? Or a recent spike in your home blood pressure readings? Or maybe you were recently prescribed a medication, and you aren't able to tolerate the side effects.

Many patients have a lengthy medical history with a multitude of concerns. However, they also have one or two acute concerns that take priority over the rest. These should be at the top of list for discussion during the appointment.

If, despite all attempts to communicate your needs and optimize your approach, you continue to feel dismissed or unheard, finding a new physician may be the next best step. As I discuss later in this book, you have full permission to do so.

A client of mine decided to seek a new cardiologist. Her current physician was becoming more dismissive of her concerns and provided a decreasing level of hope for her condition. In assisting her with this search, I found a cardiologist who recently left a larger hospital system to open a private practice.

I explained to her that this may be the best of both worlds—a cardiologist who was trained at one of the top medical centers, but who now chooses to have a smaller patient volume in his own practice. And that's exactly what we found.

Given his ability to dictate the length and quality of his visits, he learned about my client both medically and personally. In addition, she learned about his mom who lived in Spain and was struggling with progressive dementia. The seemingly simple act of asking how his mom was doing gave my client a feeling of depth to their relationship.

We were able to close the gap and meet in the gray space.

If any barriers are present, either as listed above or otherwise, identifying and addressing these before establishing care with a physician would be helpful. If Spanish is your first language, you may choose to seek a physician who is also fluent in Spanish. This would allow for fewer obstacles in communication.

If you find health literacy to be a significant concern for you, asking the physician to explain everything in simple terminology can be a helpful approach. You may also choose to be accompanied by a patient advocate who would listen and process the information in a way that can later be written down and explained.

There are many ways to optimize communication. Find what works best for you and seek assistance when necessary.

Both you and your physician deserve an opportunity to meet and connect in the gray space.

Peace Points

- Physicians are trained to communicate in concise language, sharing only what is deemed important, while patients are seeking to be seen and heard.
- The gray space between these two communication styles can be difficult to navigate.
- Peace can be found through a deep understanding of these differences and working on what is in your control.

Guided Meditation

Choose an area of your home or office that is comfortable and mostly free from distractions. Listening to what your body needs right now, you may lie flat on your back, sit with your legs crossed and your back upright, or choose another position that feels best. Close your eyes softly, or gently gaze downward if that feels better.

Start by focusing entirely on the area right underneath the point of your nose. As you inhale, notice the temperature of this area and how it may feel cool. As you exhale, take note of any changes and how it may feel warmer as the air releases back out. Sit here for another minute focusing only on that area and the changes you notice with each inhale and exhale.

Now imagine you are meeting with your physician in a completely different environment. Choose a location that normally brings you peace and joy. This may be in a cabin in the mountains, on white sand at the beach, or simply at your home. Stick with the location that comes to mind first.

Your physician greets you with a warm smile and invitation to sit down. In this environment, you have the freedom to communicate your concerns, thoughts, feelings…anything that's on your mind. Notice what comes up for you here as topics you wish to speak about. Is it symptom-specific, or is it something else? Stress? Grief? There are no right answers here, so allow your heart to speak clearly and loudly.

Imagine your physician actively listening to you while remaining present and connected. What does that feel like? What do you want in return? Continued freedom to be heard, or advice and direction? Stay here for a few more moments, asking yourself what is needed at this time.

When you are done sharing what you feel needs to be shared, thank your physician for taking the time to hear you today. Send gratitude to yourself for sharing what your heart felt was necessary.

Take a few deep breaths, reflecting back on this experience. When you're ready, slowly open your eyes. Stay curious as to what type of communication you felt was needed, and journal if you wish. I encourage you to practice this meditation before your next physician appointment as a method of self-inquiry and of achieving clarity.

CHAPTER 7

HUMANISM

The medical models have evolved from a humanistic approach to biomedical to biopsychosocial. Where compassion and empathy have been missing, data and scientific evidence have taken over. There is hope, however, and most importantly there are options for patients seeking answers.

IN the comedy-drama based on the true story of Hunter "Patch" Adams, Dean Walcott famously said, "It is human nature to lie, take shortcuts, to lose your nerve, get tired and make mistakes. No rational patient would put his trust in a human being, and we're not gonna let him! It is our mission here to rigorously and ruthlessly train the humanity out of you and make you into something better. We're gonna make doctors out of you!"

Although the movie was released in 1998, the story was set in the late 1960s or early 1970s. Dean Walcott's statement is very telling of not only the time, but of the theory that doctors should not be humans. Their training should allow them to transcend this identified state of poor decision-making and errors and ultimately become something superior.

Humanistic Model

Humanism in medicine far predated the dehumanization movement that is inherent in Dean Walcott's quote. Dating back to the fifth century BC, the Hippocratic Oath called for physicians to put the interests of patients first. The field of medicine was considered one of high morals and ethical values (Hulail 2018).[12]

Sir William Osler (1837–1901), the often-recognized father of modern medicine, is said to have mentored his students with the following advice: "Listen to the patient. He is telling you the diagnosis." He also stated, "It is much more important to know what sort of person has a disease than to know what sort of disease a person has."

Any difficulty in imagining a physician actually verbalizing Sir Osler's words is a direct result of the dehumanization that occurred several decades following his death.

The historical perspective provided in Chapter 1 outlines many of the dehumanizing factors that led, and continue to lead, to the decreasing focus on the patients' best interests, including the shift to medicine becoming a business enterprise as well as the increase in technology and decrease in appointment times with physicians.

Biomedical Model

If the humanistic model is not what patients are experiencing in modern day medicine, what model has taken its place?

The biomedical model.

Essentially, this model reduces us as human beings to that which is objective and tangible from a biological perspective. In other words, it uses scientific knowledge we have gained about the human body's normal physiological functioning and defines illness as deviations from this.

On its surface, utilizing factual, evidence-based data to determine

---

12   Hulail, "Humanism in Medical Practice," 336.

causation, diagnosis, and treatment makes sense. However, upon further evaluation, one can relatively easily find the gaps inherent in this model, specifically the inattention to psychological, spiritual, social, and environmental factors contributing to disease.

Within the medical system, physicians and other providers often use a template known by the acronym SOAP to document in a patient's electronic chart. SOAP stands for subjective, objective, assessment, plan. The assessment and plan sections, and the information they contain, are relatively self-explanatory.

The subjective and objective sections, however, may not be as obvious. The former is intended for information gained from the patient that cannot be tangibly evaluated on physical exam or testing. This usually includes their reported symptoms and complaints, such as lower back pain, extreme fatigue, or hair thinning. The latter, on the other hand, is representative of the data obtained from the patient. This often includes vital signs, such as blood pressure and heart rate, as well as lab and imaging results.

While the inclusion of that which is considered subjective is arguably important, it is not uncommon for more attention to be directed towards objective findings. For example, if a patient verbalizes that he is struggling with back pain (subjective), but the radiologist reads the scans as otherwise normal (objective), the assessment may indicate no identifiable cause for pain. The plan may consequently be a pain medication to help with what appears to be subjective-only findings.

Factors that may be missed in this biomedical approach include, but are very much not limited to, the patient's physical demands at work, his home environment and functional positioning while sitting or sleeping, and his stress level both personally and professionally.

Will the pain medication help? Possibly. Will it provide a sustainable, long-term resolution? Not likely.

Biopsychosocial Model

In an attempt to close the gaps of the biomedical model, psychiatrist and internist George Engel proposed a new model: the biopsychosocial model (Bolton 2020).[13] By reconnecting the physician to the patient's psychological and social health, this model suggests that chemistry and physics alone are insufficient to determine causation of illness.

While Engel does not equate his model entirely with humanism, he does suggest we pair our understanding of scientific principles with the human elements of medicine to achieve a broader, more holistic approach.

To fully understand a patient's diagnosis of depression, the biopsychosocial model would encourage a practitioner to consider a combination of factors, including the biology or genetics of the patient, the family dynamic and childhood development, and current and previous environmental stressors.

In other words, this model falls in alignment with Sir William Osler's quote: "A good physician treats the disease; a great physician treats the patient who has the disease."

Navigating the Models

With the number of models and approaches that have been proposed and may be in use by varying physicians, navigating the healthcare system becomes further complicated. It is rare that a physician's office declares on their website or in their lobby that their practice style is humanistic. More often, patients are left to figure this out by trial and error.

While the onus is not on the patient to change an individual physician's approach, it is helpful to understand the historical shifts in models and how a physician may approach disease diagnosis and management. Knowing that many conventional Western medicine physicians were

---

13   Bolton, "The Biopsychosocial Model," 13.

trained and therefore practice under the biomedical model allows you as a patient to realize the limitations that may be inherent in their approach.

If your lab work is otherwise within normal limits and additional testing is negative, your subjective symptoms may be either dismissed or misunderstood under the biomedical model. You may begin to question whether your symptoms are real or simply *in your head* as there is an apparent mismatch between how you feel and what your biology shows. However, understanding that the biomedical model is not equipped to optimally help you in this scenario may instead lead you to seek another provider who takes a more biopsychosocial or humanistic approach.

Functional medicine practitioners, for example, often review every decade of a patient's life to identify physical and psychological events that may be contributing to symptoms many years later. This extreme attention to the gaps inherent in the biomedical model is largely why this field has increased exponentially in popularity.

I personally sought the expertise of a functional medicine physician to help me optimize my health from its current state. She was trained as a conventional medical doctor and then later chose to apply functional medicine to her approach with patients.

Our initial appointment was approximately an hour and a half. She asked me to recall emotions and events from each decade of my life, starting from zero to ten years of age. She wanted me to include everything from my home environment to psychological stressors as well as health-related concerns.

The thought process is that childhood physical or emotional trauma, or recurrent illness, may play a role in the body's inability to perform optimally many years later. And if we don't identify and address these factors, we are missing the mark entirely in our attempt to diagnose and treat.

During my personal recollection of each decade, I found it difficult to identify anything of significance. My family dynamic was loving and supportive, my living conditions were safe and clean, and my health was relatively good. I did recall being a perfectionist and therefore was stressed most of my academic career, which she definitely took into account during her evaluation.

Some of the red flags that can be discovered in this process include possible mold exposure, toxin overload from recurrent bacterial or viral infections, and unhealed physical or psychological trauma. All are factors that are largely ignored in the biomedical model.

As my physician continued to ask questions, it became clear that my gastrointestinal tract was not performing optimally. I had a long-standing history of gastritis symptoms since I was a young adult, which I attributed to the overuse of anti-inflammatory medications for frequent headaches. Although these symptoms had become normal for me, she believed there was an underlying cause not yet identified.

As a result, she ordered bloodwork and a stool sample. I fully expected both to be normal with a possible need to supplement with probiotics.

I was shocked when the results showed I had *H. Pylori*, a bacterium that is known to cause stomach ulcers, and a parasite. Both of these microorganisms could have caused my body more damage over time if they had remained unidentified and untreated.

In the biomedical model, there was no significant indication to order these types of tests. My symptoms were well controlled, with only occasional flare-ups. I had undergone a few upper endoscopies, which showed redness and inflammation but no ulcers or other concerns. Therefore, from an objective standpoint, I was clear. I was even arguably clear from a subjective standpoint as I rarely brought these infrequent symptoms up during appointments.

But my functional medicine physician wanted to know why. Why was I experiencing frequent headaches at a young age that then led me to take anti-inflammatory medications? Why did I have symptoms of stomach irritation, even if infrequently?

The number of times she asked *why* was both surprising and refreshing.

She hypothesized that my childhood dental mercury fillings were possibly contributing to my ongoing headaches. Under her advice, I sought a holistic dentist who safely removed those fillings. Since that time, my headaches have been mostly nonexistent.

I also started on a three-month supplement regimen to address the microorganisms that were identified and to rebuild my gut health. I continue to be surprised by how much better I feel and how unlikely it would have been under the biomedical model to have these issues addressed.

While my personal experience is not intended to be a prescription for anyone else, it hopefully highlights how the different approaches and models can not only provide you hope but also tangible answers and solutions.

Re-Humanizing Medicine

At the heart of the movement to rehumanize medicine is the Arnold P. Gold Foundation, a not-for-profit organization established in 1988 by Arnold Gold, MD; Sandra Gold, EdD; and their colleagues at the Columbia University College of Physicians and Surgeons in New York ("The Arnold P. Gold Foundation," n.d.).[14] As a world-renowned pediatric neurologist, Dr. Gold and his wife sought to nurture and preserve the tradition of the caring physician.

Dr. Gold defines humanism in healthcare as "a respectful and compassionate relationship between physicians, as well as other members of the healthcare team, and their patients." He further states that "it reflects attitudes and behaviors that are sensitive to the values and the cultural and ethnic backgrounds of others." To Dr. Gold and his team, the humanistic physician demonstrates integrity, excellence, collaboration and compassion, altruism, respect and resilience, empathy, and service.

Humanism Research

In true evidence-based medicine fashion, many researchers have sought to study the impacts of a doctor's empathy level on patient outcomes.

---

14   The Arnold P. Gold Foundation, Accessed April 5, 2023, https://www.gold-foundation.org.

A systematic review was conducted to investigate the link between physicians' or nurses' empathy and patient outcomes in cancer care (Lelorain et al. 2012).[15] Researchers found that clinicians' empathy was related to higher patient satisfaction and lower distress.

This link between empathy and clinical outcomes has been studied on a relatively large scale with commonly diagnosed health conditions. Over twenty thousand diabetic patients in Italy were studied retrospectively, and researchers found that the patients of physicians with high empathy scores, compared with patients of physicians with moderate and low empathy scores, had a significantly lower rate of acute metabolic complications (Canale et al. 2012).[16] In short, the more empathy a physician showed to a patient, the less likely that patient would experience complications from the disease, including hyperosmolar state, diabetic ketoacidosis, and coma.

In a prospective randomized clinical trial, researchers studied over seven hundred patients with the common cold (Rakel et al. 2011).[17] When the patient perceived that the clinician was empathetic, the severity and length of the cold were significantly less. The impact of this was further shown in objective measures, such as immune markers in lab work. In this study, the researchers looked specifically at immune-related cells known as neutrophils, a type of white blood cell, and interleukin-8 (IL-8), a cytokine that attracts and activates neutrophils.

In your personal health journey, you may be familiar with lab work that shows your total white blood cell count. This is a more macro-level look at how strong or weak your immune system may be at any given time. It also provides a quantitative measurement for clinicians to identify a possible infection.

It is clear that humanism in medicine is not simply a good idea on paper. It has been proven to improve patients' health.

---

15   Lelorain et al., "A Systematic Review," 1255–64.

16   Canale et al., "The Relationship Between Physician Empathy and Disease Complications," 1243–49.

17   Rakel et al., "Perception of Empathy in the Therapeutic Encounter," 390–97.

Future Medical Models

I certainly don't claim to be an *intuitive* or have the ability to predict the future. However, I believe the public's demand for an increase in attention and compassion from their physicians, combined with the growing understanding of the mind-body connection, will fuel a return to humanism. Or at least result in a clear preference of the biopsychosocial model's acknowledgment of the interplay of human elements in disease processes.

I don't think it's in question that patients want a deeper, more empathetic connection with their doctors. It's also true that the vast majority of doctors chose the medical field to help others. When these two realities are allowed to intersect organically and without interruption from corporate entities, healthcare will reach its optimal state.

Until then, I encourage you to find the physician and model that serves your needs the best. And if you need help with the permission part, I have you covered in the next chapter.

Peace Points

- Humanism in medicine dates back at least to the fifth century BC.

- Although the biomedical model took over, there is a slow return to humanistic medicine with the development of the biopsychosocial model.

- Until physicians are given the time and space to practice medicine with the empathy and compassion with which they entered the field, patients must seek understanding of the current landscape to find the care approach they need.

CHAPTER 8

PERMISSION

The medical system and our associated belief systems lead us to make decisions that may not be aligned with our values and wishes. Until we are able to give ourselves permission to act outside of the status quo, it can be helpful if someone who has worked inside the system grants us that permission.

THE US healthcare system moves quickly.

And honestly, we, as consumers of that care, expect it to.

We are blessed with abundant resources in this country that allow us to schedule an imaging or blood test within days, sometimes hours, of it being ordered. In many cities, a referral to a specialist can be sent, received, and a new nonurgent appointment scheduled within days to weeks.

This is not the case in other countries around the world. Canada, for example, has been identified as having some of the longest wait times for specialty care in the world (Liddy 2020).[18] In a retrospective study of over two thousand Canadian referral charts, 11 percent had no documentation of being seen within a year of the referral being placed.

---

18 Liddy, "How Long Are Canadians Waiting," 438.

In addition, the referrals labeled as "urgent" had a median wait time of twenty-four days, with the upper limit resting at seventy-one days.

Why does this matter? Shouldn't the quickness with which our medical system moves be considered an unequivocal positive? *Yes.* And *no.* In emergent and urgent cases, the response time is often life-altering. When my father was diagnosed with lymphoma, he was also found to have a ruptured spleen that was directly causing his excruciating abdominal pain. His life depended on his spleen being surgically removed quickly. And due to the availability of resources, it was. Had he resided in another country or a more rural part of the US, the blood loss from his broken spleen could have resulted in a much earlier death. Surgeons performing emergent life-saving surgery are heroes indeed. His splenectomy gave us another year of cherished memories, for which I will be eternally grateful.

After his surgery, we then faced the lymphoma diagnosis. Although there was no way to know how long cancer cells had been multiplying in his body by this point, the assumption by his medical team was years. It was certainly long enough to spread to his spleen and cause it to burst. This apparent long-standing disease was not considered emergent or urgent. No treatment or procedure would be lifesaving if given or performed in the next several hours.

Out of the options he was offered, none included time.

He was rushed to biopsy various lymph nodes with minimal informed consent or explanation. The understood yet never verbalized agreement was that the vulnerable patient needed medical care, and the providers of the medical care would proceed as they knew best.

At this point in my life and career, I didn't know what I didn't know.

I was a product of the very system that was moving forward full speed ahead, and the wisdom I would later gain was still years away. The medical team was doing exactly what I expected them to do, which was rush to diagnosis so they could then sprint towards a chemotherapy treatment plan. My dad was never granted permission to understand the basis of the diagnosis, the scientific evidence of efficacy and safety of the treatment plan, or the existence of alternative modalities that could be offered outside the system. More importantly, neither he nor I granted ourselves that permission.

This, my friends, is what I hope to give you in this chapter and throughout the book—*permission.*

Permission to be confident in your expertise in what it's like to live in your body.

Permission to step outside the relationship norms of the medical system and ask questions.

Permission to pause.

Permission to take a day, or several, to consider the treatment approach being recommended and to decide whether it aligns with your goals and wishes.

Permission to have goals and wishes.

Could you give this permission to yourself? Absolutely, and I encourage you to do so. But I also acknowledge that if I struggled with this, it's probable that many of you do as well. Until you're able to take the permission baton and run independently with it, allow me to hold it for you.

Even if just for a short while.

Permission to Ask Questions

There are many questions you are likely already comfortable asking your medical team.

"Is that medication or procedure covered under my insurance?"

"When do you want to see me next?"

"When can I return to work?"

"Do I need to fast for my blood work?"

These questions roll off your tongue and require no permission. The physician expects them and can answer quickly and easily. In addition, the system has taught you that these questions are acceptable.

I want to discuss the questions that are taboo, unexpected, and when asked, may verbally demonstrate your healthy level of skepticism. As you work on developing this new habit of curiosity and questioning, allow me to provide some starting point suggestions.

Permission to Question Your Diagnosis

A client of mine, who we will call Maria, was facing a diagnosis of lupus, which is an inflammatory condition in which the immune system attacks itself and causes hallmark symptoms such as joint pain and skin rashes. Her labs were so confirmatory they could have been taken directly out of the lupus chapter in a medical school textbook.

Maria's physicians immediately decided she had lupus and referred her to a rheumatologist for next steps in treatment. Prior to heading down that path, we decided to ask questions.

"Can the ANA test be elevated in conditions other than lupus?"

"How common is it for a true lupus patient to have none of the hallmark symptoms?"

"Is it possible these labs do indeed confirm that her immune system is dealing with something, but that *thing* may not be lupus?"

These questions may at first feel intimidating if you're not accustomed to asking them or knowing how to formulate them. This will take time and practice, much like anything else in life we seek to master. But the results are well worth the effort. Until you feel comfortable with more complex questions, try simplifying this to "How possible is it that the diagnosis is incorrect?" and base subsequent questions on the answers received.

Maria and I found a physician who was willing to consider an expanded list of possible diagnoses and confirmed that it was unlikely lupus was the answer. How did this impact her? A visit to the rheumatologist and the associated medications that would have been prescribed became unnecessary, at least for the time being.

Questioning a diagnosis isn't just important in theory or via anecdotal stories. Accrediting healthcare entities in the US, such as the Joint Commission, track medical errors, including those that are a result of an incorrect diagnosis. The current estimates show that forty thousand to eighty thousand patients suffer harm or death due to diagnostic errors each year. The overall misdiagnosis rate is 10–15 percent, meaning between one and two out of every ten patients will statistically be given an inaccurate diagnosis (Rodziewicz 2022).[19]

In case you need one additional nudge of permission, let's break down the word *diagnosis*. It is derived from the Greek words *gnosis*, which means "knowledge," and *dia*, which means "between." Stated another way, diagnosing a patient is intended to involve an "in between" of "knowledge" involving both physician and patient.

We have already established the extensive knowledge gained by physicians during their didactic and clinical training. And I hope I have effectively made the case in the discussion on unlearning that you are indeed an expert on *you*. Therefore, your active engagement in your medical care, including the diagnosis stage, is vitally important. Your curiosity and willingness to ask questions, especially those about your diagnosis, may very well save your life.

Permission to Take Time

How can a system that prides itself on quick action also value the importance of pausing?

It doesn't.

At least not very well.

To my knowledge, there's no course or module in medical school that trains budding new physicians on giving patients space and time to make the decision that's best for them. There's no peer-reviewed treatment

---

19   Rodziewicz, Hipskind, and Houseman, "Medical Error Reduction and Prevention."

guideline that lists "time to think" as a recommended first-line approach. Physician offices don't have dedicated space labeled "compassion room" to allow patients to process diagnostic or prognostic information in a peaceful, non-sterile environment.

No space. No time.

Just as our society is built on hustle culture, the medical system is judged as unproductive or even negligent if it doesn't move as quickly as possible. Like riding a train that's not intending to stop, jumping off to breathe can feel intimidating and almost more harmful than staying the course.

My friend, whom I will call Laura, shared with me that all she wanted when she received her breast cancer diagnosis was time. This diagnosis was unexpected and shocking as she felt otherwise well. She understood that waiting a few days or a week to make a treatment decision would not likely impact her long-term chances of success.

But the physicians wanted an answer.

And her family desperately wanted her to live, which they equated with following the doctors' advice and timeline.

With pressure from all sides, she quieted her inner wisdom and moved forward with chemotherapy. Several years later, she still regretted not giving herself the space and time she desired. While not commonly discussed within the Western medical system, Laura knew other less-toxic treatment approaches existed. She felt drawn to explore these options as they focused on supporting the body's innate healing, which is in direct opposition to the fight-and-kill focus of chemotherapy.

Would she have decided the same treatment course? Maybe. But making that decision out of fear and a sense of urgency did not feel aligned to her.

How do you create space to breathe and think when the medical system is moving at full speed? You simply *do*. Or more accurately, you allow yourself the grace to *not do*, for whatever time period you need. If you don't require urgent or emergent lifesaving treatment, the time you need to make the decision that's best for you is fully under your control.

If your physician orders a biopsy in three days, but you need more time to understand the procedure and its risks, you may choose to ask for a follow-up appointment to discuss your questions and concerns. If the rheumatologist gives you a prescription for two new medications that are known to suppress your immune system, you have permission to hold onto those prescriptions until you have the information you need to make a decision.

In other words, remember your reframing of this relationship, specifically as consultant and consultee. You obtained one expert's opinion. Any and all next steps are in your decision-making power as the consultee.

Permission to Have Health-Related Goals

You have likely filled out countless medical intake forms throughout your adult life. The seemingly endless topics include your family history, personal medical history, allergies, current medications, referring physician, and many others. One important question these forms fail to ask a vast majority of the time is, "What are your top three health-related goals?" In fact, it is so unlikely you have been asked this that you may be considering this question for the very first time right now.

We identify and evaluate goals in many other areas of our lives, including jobs, businesses, and legal matters. Our health, however, often takes a back seat until we are forced to move it to the front.

Allow me to give you permission to have goals for your health and express these goals to your medical team. Furthermore, I encourage you to expand these goals beyond your legal wishes. Working with an estate attorney to develop an advance directive, such as a living will, is extremely important. The medical system acknowledges this and will often help you develop one if you haven't consulted an attorney.

Your goals, however, are not limited to lifesaving treatments or assigning a healthcare surrogate. They are developed as a result of asking yourself questions you may have not considered before now.

What do you value more from a physician—training from a top institution or a compassionate bedside manner?

Does seeing a physician in person feel more valuable to you than utilizing telehealth options?

Do you prefer a holistic approach to your health, or would you rather maximize the options science has developed over the last several decades?

Are you seeking to travel the world, or is your primary goal to feel well enough to play with your grandchildren at home?

The key here is there are no right or wrong questions or answers. Your goals are yours to own and work toward. If you verbalize them to one of your physicians and you are met with resistance or dismissiveness, the next question to ask isn't how to change your goals to make your doctor happy. Rather, ask yourself if seeking a new, more open-minded physician feels like the best next step—one who hears you, validates you, and ultimately works with you to help you accomplish your goals.

This, of course, leads us to the next topic of permission, which is deserving of its own subsection.

Permission to Change Physicians

Many of my clients find it difficult to make the decision to change doctors. They often feel a sense of loyalty and responsibility to do everything in their power to make it work, much like other relationships they value in life. There's also an element of familiarity, such that starting a new relationship feels overwhelming. In fact, continuing in their comfort zone, regardless of how poorly it is serving them, becomes preferred over exploring the unknown.

Don't worry; I'm here to help you with this important mindset shift.

A helpful starting point for this topic, and honestly any other area of permission with which you may need assistance, is the method developed by Byron Kathleen Mitchell, better known as Byron Katie. A speaker, author, and spiritual guide to many, Byron Katie encourages a process of self-inquiry, called The Work, that involves asking four simple questions about beliefs we hold that may be causing us to struggle (Katie 2003).[20]

Is it true?

Can you absolutely know that it's true?

How do you react when you believe that thought?

Who would you be without that thought?

The best way to expand this is to practice with an example.

Let's assume you want to change your primary care physician as she has increasingly become distant, distracted, and impersonal during appointments. You feel torn because you've been going to her for fifteen years and leaving her practice may make her sad and angry with you. This misalignment, namely wanting to leave but choosing not to, is causing you anxiety, so you decide to lean on Byron Katie's work.

Is it true that your decision to leave her practice will make her sad and angry? For the answer to be an unequivocal yes, a conversation would have had to occur. Since you've never discussed this with her, your answer has to be no.

Can you absolutely know that it's true? No, not without directly asking her and her honest response being affirmative to your belief.

How do you react when you believe she will be sad and angry with you if you choose to find a new doctor? Maybe you experience increased anxiety and frustration that you are still going to a clinic where you don't feel heard or seen. Maybe you continue to make decisions out of fear that you are upsetting a member of your healthcare team.

Who would you be without that thought? In the absence of this belief, you would be free from anxiety and willing to find a new doctor that better fits your needs. In addition, you would be open to telling her how you feel so she can use that feedback to evaluate her care approach with other patients.

Simple, right? Byron Katie intended it to be.

---

20   Katie, *Loving What Is: Four Questions That Can Change Your Life.*

For those of you who are more analytical and statistics-oriented, allow me to provide one more reason to grant yourself this permission. Traditional primary care physicians often work under a panel of patients, meaning a list of people who are assigned to their care. This panel can be anywhere from fifteen hundred patients to upwards of four thousand patients. Effectively this means that if you are the first patient to leave a physician who cares for four thousand patients, that physician has lost 0.025 percent of the assigned panel.

While I wholeheartedly believe physicians are caring people who want the best for their patients, the reality is a vast majority would not even notice if their list suddenly decreased by 0.025 percent. Yes, the office staff may receive a medical records request from your new physician and may make notation in your chart, but that's as far as it will go.

Trust me.

Or better yet, trust the statistics and grant yourself permission to find a physician who not only meets your needs but exceeds your expectations.

Permission to Accept Your Mortality

From a young age, many of us are taught to run away from death. Our parents may have encouraged this by shielding us from funerals, avoiding discussions on end-of-life planning, or explicitly stating phrases like, "Don't worry; I'm not dying." I personally recall having a deep fear at the age of five that I would be all alone if my parents died.

While our culture in America views death as a tragedy, other cultures, such as in Mexico, make it a tradition each year to celebrate the lives of those who passed in what is known as the "Day of the Dead," or *el Dia de los Muertos*. In effect, whether we choose to run away from death or reframe death as an opportunity to celebrate life, the inevitability of death for each of us remains.

Physicians are taught to do no harm, and ultimately save the lives of those who are in their care. If a patient entrusted to them dies, it often feels like a failure, even if the patient was in critical condition with a poor prognosis. Combining our cultural aversion to death with our medical system's goal of winning the fight against death, it can seem like an impossible or even illogical mindset shift to accept this reality.

Just as we have worked on unlearning other belief systems, we can unlearn our subconscious belief that death should be feared and avoided at all costs. This doesn't mean we should seek death or desire it. But our resistance to an undeniable fact that we will indeed all die is arguably causing an unnecessary amount of turmoil and stress, neither of which has any positive return on investment.

As we individually grant ourselves permission to accept our mortality, we open the door to have more meaningful conversations with our family and our physicians. We can face the need for end-of-life planning and reframe it as a way to help those we love rather than surrendering our will to live.

Watching my dad at the end of his life was both heartbreaking and beautiful. With an amazing amount of courage and acceptance, he made phone calls to his friends to express his gratitude and ultimately say his final goodbyes. He gave himself permission to stop resisting and find peace in his mortality.

I visited an intuitive a few months after my dad passed and her language still brings me peace to this day. She said, "Your dad died because his body could no longer support the creations of his soul."

And thus began my own process of accepting death.

Peace Points

- The US medical system moves at a fast pace, giving us little space and time to evaluate recommended treatment options.
- You have permission to do what is best for you.

- This includes, but is not limited to, asking your physician tough questions, taking the time you need to make a decision, creating personal health-related goals, and changing doctors as you feel it is necessary.

Guided Meditation

Find an area of your home or office that is comfortable and mostly free from distractions. Sit upright or lie down, respecting your body's preference in this moment. Close your eyes softly, or gently gaze downward if that feels better.

Begin by placing your right hand on your heart and your left hand over your right. Feel your heart beating underneath your palms. Notice your chest rise and fall with each breath and begin to imagine your breath originating from your heart, right beneath your hands. Stay here for five more breaths.

Now, think of an area in your life, specifically related to your health, that feels stressful. Maybe it's because you are seeking answers and not getting them. Maybe it's a misaligned energy with one of your physicians. Again, there's no right answers in meditation—only what comes up for you. As you dig deeper into this area, ask your heart what is needed here. Do you need to make a decision? Do you need to surrender to something out of your control? Is your heart asking you to have a difficult conversation with someone involved in your care?

Once you have clarity over what may need to happen, imagine a beam of light starting from the center of your heart leading directly into the palms of your hands. This beam is a symbol of connection and support. Notice the color of this beam. Observe how brightly it shines.

As you sit here for a few minutes allowing this beam to fill the space between your heart and your hands, send it gratitude for the reminder that it's always available to you when you need it. The reminder that permission lies inside of you.

Take a few more deep breaths and allow your hands to gently fall back to your lap or the floor beneath you. Allow your senses to feel the room you are in and the surface you are sitting or lying on.

And when you're ready, slowly open your eyes.

CHAPTER 9

SUPPORT

People need people. And while the medical system can make us feel isolated and alone, there are ways to identify and seek the help and support you need.

What Society and Science Tell Us About Human Connection

J**UST** do it."

"You got this."

"Every man for himself."

Corporate and societal language have taught us in many ways to believe we are walking this earth alone, and as such, the onus is on each of us to figure it all out. At least once we hit the wise and capable age of eighteen.

It is, therefore, understandable that upon facing a new medical diagnosis, we immediately feel the entirety of the burden on our shoulders. We believe it's our battle to fight and win as a single soldier army. We got this. Or more accurately, *you* got this.

The good news? There is an abundance of scientific literature debunking what we have been taught, effectively reminding us that people do indeed need people.

One landmark study published in 1988 demonstrated the significance of social relationships on health (House 1988).[21] The researchers found that the lack of social connection is more harmful to our health than obesity, smoking, and high blood pressure.

A meta-analysis of over three hundred thousand participants across 148 studies showed a 50 percent increased likelihood of survival for participants with stronger social relationships (Holt-Lunstad 2010).[22] The impact shown by a lack of social relationships on the risk of death was comparable to well-established risk factors, such as smoking and alcohol consumption.

Researchers in the UK conducted a systematic review and meta-analysis of over thirty-five thousand records investigating the association between loneliness or social isolation and the incidence of coronary heart disease (CHD) and stroke (Valtorta 2015).[23] Their results not only confirmed the association we knew to be true but quantified it. Poor social relationships were associated with a 29 percent increase in the risk of CHD and a 32 percent increase in the risk of stroke.

Fast forward to the COVID-19 pandemic, and social connection (or the extreme lack thereof experienced during that time) became a hot topic. In fact, researchers gave socializing its own labeled vitamin: Vitamin S. While the world was figuring out how to contain a virus, sick patients were forced to sit alone in emergency rooms with masks on, making communication that much more difficult. Families were visiting loved ones in skilled nursing facilities by waving and smiling, while masked, on the other side of a pane of glass. Many patients died

---

21   House, Landis, and Umberson, "Social Relationships and Health," 540.

22   Holt-Lunstad, Smith, and Layton, "Social Relationships and Mortality Risk," 4.

23   Valtorta et al., "Loneliness and Social Isolation as Risk Factors," 1014.

alone while others said their goodbyes by shedding tears over streaming software programs like Zoom.

As we enter a post-pandemic era, many state officials are realizing the trauma and detriment this caused both physically and emotionally. Laws have been set into motion in some states to ensure no patient is forced to die alone. The extreme social distancing and the resultant mental harm it caused has led to a renewed emphasis on *people needing people*.

But what if you are a self-identified introvert? What if you enjoy and actually feel more energized with time alone? What if your circle of friends and family is small in perspective to others you know?

There's more good news!

Feeling socially connected is just that—a subjective feeling of connection. It is less about the absolute number of people to whom you are connected than it is about how deep you feel your connection is to those people.

Quality over quantity. Now there's a societal phrase that actually makes sense!

Why Do We Struggle to Ask for Support?

Some of you may be thinking, "Well, that's all well and good. We need friends; got it. I have plenty of friends. My issue is asking those friends for help when I need it."

I hear you. And you're not alone.

Support means to "hold up." How do we ask someone to hold us up when we feel like we're falling? How do we burden someone we love with our needs when they are likely dealing with their own struggles?

Before we answer the *how*, it's helpful to understand the *why*. Why do we avoid asking for help? Why do we identify ourselves as being a burden if we do ask? There are a multitude of reasons this may be the case.

Maybe you're a giver. Your friends and family know you as such, and it's hard for you to move to the position of recipient. It feels awkward or, to some, even unethical to receive.

Maybe your family taught you to be independent and leave the house the minute you turned eighteen. You've held that value all your life, and asking for support feels like dependency, which you feel is the antithesis of everything you were taught.

Maybe you have a difficult time trusting people. Whether it's based on personal experience or from consuming fear-inducing content produced by the media, you might find yourself not able to trust another person to help you the way you need it.

Whatever your *why* is, identifying it is progress. If you feel the reasoning behind your inability to ask for support has deep roots, working with a therapist could be a reasonable next step. If you feel it is due to a belief system that can relatively easily be unlearned, I would encourage you to work on that. As I described in the previous chapter, using Byron Katie's self-inquiry may be helpful here.

During a coaching session with a client, we decided to focus on social support. She mentioned that her two daughters were her life. They lived two hours away from her, and she desperately wanted a closer relationship with them.

When I asked why they didn't talk on the phone or visit more often, she stated that she didn't want to be a bother to them. They were both adults now and had their own lives. She felt that her cancer diagnosis would place unnecessary stress on them.

I encouraged her to use Byron Katie's approach to investigate this further. When I asked her if it was true that her daughters felt she was a burden, she was unable to identify evidence of this. They had never verbalized this to her or appeared to be actively avoiding her. Once she was able to realize this was a story in her mind and not a truth in reality, she was able to break through her own barrier and reach out. In the following four weeks, she wrote letters to them, spoke on the phone multiple times, and even visited with the oldest.

Help Them Help You

"We are all just walking each other home." This quote from spiritual leader Ram Dass is my favorite reminder of the work we are all effectively doing.

Each of us is walking a path that has been paved by someone before us. Those of us who might be creating a new path are doing so with the wisdom and instruction gained by our ancestors. They walked us home, and we are now doing the same for younger generations.

By incorporating this quote into our healthcare journey, it helps us to remember how we have walked with others when they were sick. I personally remember helping my grandmother with my grandfather when he was home on hospice. He had advanced stage Parkinson's disease and was bedbound. He was also over six feet tall and towered over his wife's osteoporotic small frame, which made seemingly small tasks much larger than they would otherwise be.

You likely also have memories of times you helped a family member or friend when they needed to be "held up." Now the challenge is for you to allow others to do the same for you. To walk *you* home.

Teach Others How to Help You

"I am so sorry you're going through this. How can I help?"

"I'm OK, but thank you for checking in."

Does this sound like a conversation you've had in the past? A friend or family member reaches out to offer help, but you're too overwhelmed with the situation to devise a help strategy? Or your quick reflex to turn down help is fueled by a desire to avoid overburdening others with a situation that you feel may not be positioned for help.

I've been there. Done that. On both the giving and receiving end of these statements.

An important lesson I learned when my dad was sick was that people don't know *how* to help you. But that doesn't mean they don't *want* to help you. In fact, it's quite the opposite. And science even backs it. Helping others triggers the release of oxytocin, a neurochemical that has powerful effects on the brain and body. It also counteracts the stress hormone cortisol. In other words, allowing others to help you ends up helping *them* as well.

A good friend of mine, who was older and wiser, taught me a great deal about this concept when my dad was dying. She called me and said, "I'm getting you and your family sandwiches so you don't have to worry about cooking lunch. Give me your order and I'll have it delivered to you."

I paused in both shock over her level of confident giving and my relief in knowing our next meal was taken care of. After expressing my gratitude, I was in awe at the impact this had on all of us. We didn't have to figure out *how* she could help us or feel like a burden for even affirmatively answering her request to help. All we had to do was choose turkey or roast beef.

And that's literally all we had left in us at that point anyway.

Not everyone has gained this level of helpful assertiveness in their giving approach. As a result, you may have to help others help you. You likely won't be taking regular inventory of your needs while you or a loved one is sick. However, you will certainly need a meal—three a day, in fact. That can be a simple way for someone to help.

Other ideas are helping pick your kids up from school, going grocery shopping, or contributing to a house cleaning service. If you have friends or family who want to get more involved in your medical care, you can consider asking them to accompany you to appointments, help take notes while you're there, or organize paperwork and medical records.

Whatever you feel would be most helpful, the point here is to *accept the offer to help* and *provide guidance on the how*. They want to walk you home. Remember, oxytocin.

So allow them.

Teach Doctors How to Help You

In chapter 1, I reviewed the medical system and how it trains new physicians. I also pointed out some areas that are lacking in sufficient academic instruction, such as nutrition. In a similar way, physicians are not taught how to incorporate coaching principles in their interview style. A coach asks open-ended, thought-provoking questions, which ultimately guide the "coachee" to make decisions and take action.

It would be a rare and unusual office visit that included coaching-style questioning from your physician, eliciting a deeper understanding of your support needs and how to ask for help. Not saying never, but don't hold your breath.

It stands to reason, then, that your physician often does not fully understand the ways in which you need support. To be clear, I don't fault them for that. If an individual physician holds a patient panel of four thousand, it would be impossible to identify and keep track of everyone's unstated needs.

How, then, can we get the support we seek from our physicians? First, we need clarity on what we need from them. This can be, and often is, the most difficult part. Just as difficult is believing that a healthcare system with a pattern of not meeting your needs would suddenly be ready and willing to do so. That's why I created the Guided Meditation at the end of this chapter to help you.

Second, we need both the courage and confidence to ask for this newly identified area of support. That includes remembering to ask, which can be accomplished by bringing a prepared list of questions to your appointment.

Do you need a therapist who specializes in medical diagnostics and management to help you process a diagnosis you received?

Did this physician recently refer you to a specialist with whom you don't feel supported, and you want to discuss alternative options?

Would a deeper discussion of the previously mentioned treatment plan help you decide if you want to proceed?

Whatever your needs may be for further medical support, it's possible and likely that your physician doesn't know and cannot fulfill an unidentified or unstated need.

Also, your physician could use an extra dose of oxytocin every now and then. So, give them the opportunity to help you.

What Does it Look Like to Have Healthcare Support?

In the several years I have worked with advocacy clients, I have come to realize that many don't know what it feels or looks like to have the support they need. With no experiential precedent in this area, the assumption can often be that "better" doesn't exist.

I am here to provide hope through example.

My client, Sophia, has severe anxiety and depression. She suffered significant damage to her heart from a heart attack a few years ago. This led to heart failure and the resultant symptoms, including extreme fatigue with minimal exertion. She is elderly and lives alone, making it difficult to complete the necessary everyday tasks many of us often take for granted.

She has intentionally sought out support over the years out of necessity. Her friends and neighbors are ready and willing to drive her to medical appointments or allow her to stay overnight if her health is unstable. Her trauma-informed psychologist team is available to her anytime, day or night, even when they are traveling out of the country.

As her patient advocate, I attend her medical appointments via speakerphone to ensure our questions get asked and that each physician is aware of the others' plans. To ensure she doesn't miss any important information discussed during the appointment, I send her a detailed summary afterward. When she is in the hospital, she calls me during physician rounds so I can hear what is being discussed and intervene if necessary.

As needed, we all meet with her as a team to make sure we each know what part we are playing in her healing and how we can support each other and, ultimately, her.

We effectively call ourselves "Team Sophia."

This is not a hypothetical dramatization. It's a real-life example of the ways in which support exists and can positively impact your life and your health.

Peace Points

- Despite societal messaging, we do indeed need people.
- Begin by identifying some of the reasons you may be resistant to seeking or receiving help.
- We can help others help us—and everyone benefits in the process.

Guided Meditation

Find an area of your home or office that is comfortable and mostly free from distractions. Check in with your body and follow its lead to either sit upright or lie down. Close your eyes softly, or gently gaze downward if that feels better.

Begin by connecting to your breath. Allow a natural inhalation and exhalation, not forcing or resisting. Notice the temperature and quality of the air moving in your nostrils as you breathe in and any changes as you breathe out through your mouth. Pay attention to your heart rate and how it changes with your breath. After a few naturally paced breaths, begin to deepen and lengthen both the inhale and exhale, noticing a more significant rise and fall in your chest. Also notice any change to the rate of your heartbeat.

Taking a head-to-toe scan of your body. Begin by identifying any areas of tightness or tension in your forehead. Release any tendencies to squint or contract the small muscles around your eyes. Soften the muscles in your cheeks and jaw, allowing the tongue to fall from the roof of the mouth.

Bring your shoulders up, back, and down, allowing them to relax away from the ears. Release tension in the belly and allow your legs to fall naturally without tension or contraction. Anchor back into your breath if you have strayed, noticing the softness and relaxation in your body and breathing into any areas that may have retightened.

Imagine an internal small ball of light in the center of your chest. Notice its color, brightness, and intensity. Allow it to hold the qualities it wants to hold. Connect with this light as it represents your internal guidance and wisdom. If it wants to grow bigger, allow it to expand. If it prefers to stay small and dense, appreciate its contained beauty.

Staying connected to your breath, ask this light, your inner wisdom, what it needs right now. Allow it to answer in words, sounds, symbols, or otherwise. Receive the response, even if unexpected.

Does your body need more movement? More rest?

Is your body asking for more nutrient-dense foods?

Do you need to seek more growth opportunities or possibly slow down after recently pursuing a new degree?

Allow any and all answers to come and receive them with an open heart and mind.

Now, ask this ball of light what support it needs from others.

You may see a vision of specific people in your life. Or your inner wisdom may point out concerns that are becoming difficult to handle alone.

Are you being encouraged to reach out to a particular friend? Or possibly join a peer support group?

If you find your "thinking mind" trying to take over, guide your focus and attention back to the ball of light in your chest. Reanchor to your breath. Re-soften areas of your body that have tightened.

Try to feel the responses from your inner wisdom. What does it feel like to give your body what it needs? How does your heart respond to asking for and accepting help and support from others? Sit with those feelings for a minute or so.

Take a few more deep, extended breaths. Thank your inner wisdom for showing up and sharing. Begin to wiggle your fingers and toes. Feel the surface beneath you. Notice the sounds and temperature of the room you are in.

And when you are ready, slowly open your eyes.

If you have time, grab a journal and a pen and freewrite anything that came up during your meditation. If not, bring your hands to prayer position at your chest and end your meditation in a state of gratitude.

CHAPTER 10

ALLY

Society teaches us to fight. Fight our bodies, fight our medical team, fight our medical condition. But what if we flipped the script and sought allies instead?

THE entertainment industry has written the quintessential script for decades—good guy versus bad guy. The former fights for justice and morality; the latter fights for freedom and anarchy. And ultimately they fight each other while the audience attempts to predict which character will be victorious.

World history has set this same stage countless times as well. Wars between and among countries end in freedom for some and control of others.

The winner versus loser game plays out in many other areas of life, including sports, job promotions, and gambling, to name a few. It therefore isn't too much of a stretch of the imagination to see how this dichotomy has woven itself into healthcare.

When my dad was diagnosed with lymphoma, I fell into this plot quickly. I was convinced the only way I would save him and rise from the ashes in victory was to become the adversary. Not necessarily in my father's place, as he historically played the role of peacekeeper in all settings of life.

I had the story set: I would identify myself as the daughter who would fight until the bitter end. The only characters permitted to be on my side were my family and my father's primary care physician. All others would be my enemy. And the most hated enemy of all was the cancer raging in my dad's body.

So I armored up and got ready for battle. When I identified an error or act of negligence, I took out my weapons of anger as threats to report those responsible. I used language in both verbal and written communication that mirrored what society taught me.

Cancer picked the wrong girl.

Fight cancer.

I played the role well. But I didn't win. I couldn't celebrate victory. My father passed away despite my best efforts to fight. My clever social media posts demonstrating my unwillingness to back down are now filed away as memories. The multitude of arguments I had with my father's medical team did nothing but deepen the divide between physician and patient.

What I did gain was wisdom. I now know that my dad's medical team was never an enemy to fight. And neither was his cancer.

This may come as a shocking string of statements, so allow me to explain.

When we identify a need to fight someone or something, we are declaring that one person or thing will ultimately be the winner and the other the loser. In fact, the noun *fight* is defined as a violent confrontation or struggle. Not only will one party win and one lose, but the process to get there will be anything but pleasant.

Anyone who has dealt with a life-threatening diagnosis is aware of the struggle that comes with simply facing that reality. In the aftermath of receiving this news, most people are bombarded by messages from family, friends, and society encouraging them to "enter the ring."

You got this.

You will win this fight.

F*&% cancer.

So they put on their new boxing gloves, and they get ready to fight.

But they're tired. Not feeling well. Confused over their diagnosis, prognosis, and what this journey will look like. Unsure of whom or what they're fighting. Still, they are being encouraged to fight. So they do. Much like a shorter boxer swinging at his taller opponent and finding him to be just out of reach.

The physiological impact on the body from the fight approach is actually counterproductive. This heightened cortisol state of fight-or-flight mode slows down our digestion and our immune system, as if we were running from or fighting a wild animal that's chasing us. A suppressed immune system in turn gives us *less* of a fighting chance against the illness.

What if we changed the script?

What if we were no longer fighting, but seeking harmony and common ground?

What if the characters were allies rather than enemies?

To be an ally is to combine or unite with another for mutual benefit. What if you could unite with your medical team rather than fight against them? And what if a shift in perspective around the actual diagnosis could turn it into a mutually beneficial messenger rather than a force of opposition? In other words, we change the scene of our life's movie from "main character receives a diagnosis then fights with everyone including herself" to "main character receives an educated medical opinion from a physician and uses it as an indicator light that something she is thinking, doing, or being needs to be brought back into alignment to optimize healing."

I acknowledge and validate this is a significant mindset shift. Ultimately, it requires us to revisit the chapter on unlearning. You may recall the connection of dots from that chapter, which applies to this concept as well. Healing the body . . . requires fighting a war. Or so we've been taught.

I interviewed Chris Wark for my podcast in November 2020. He is a young adult cancer survivor, bestselling author, and patient advocate.

He has since become one of the most well-known cancer survivors on the planet. One of my favorite parts of his journey and message is that illness, in his case cancer, is here to teach us something.

He encourages people to not feel like victims of their circumstance or innocent bystanders of poor genetic makeup. Instead, he advises those facing this diagnosis to evaluate the diet and lifestyle decisions they've made in the past and begin making radical changes. This includes stress, negative emotions, and unhappiness as well.

The dot he inspires us to begin connecting is this: Cancer (or another life-threatening disease) . . . is a divine tap on the shoulder to help us make necessary changes.

If we follow the path Chris is suggesting, we begin to see sickness as a messenger. An ally sending us a warning signal that something needs to change. In everyday terms, it is the yellow traffic light that gently asks us to use caution and begin changing our speed to avoid potential danger ahead.

These messages don't use language as we know it. They don't speak or use written communication. Instead, they are like what Oprah Winfrey describes as *whispers*—a slight nudge that something is out of alignment. If left unanswered, the whispers become screams and eventually bricks to the head. So the earlier we can identify our allies and heed their warnings, the more likely we are to avoid their natural crescendo.

How do we make friends with our sick bodies and begin moving away from the fight club that society is ready to enroll us in? This takes time and intentionality, but it's absolutely possible. Like many other areas in our lives, it may require you to surround yourself with a different set of people.

Jim Rohn, the famous entrepreneur, author, and mentor to celebrity life coach Tony Robbins, once said, "You are the average of the five people you spend the most time with." If those five people are ready to be soldiers in your war, you will naturally take on a fight mentality. If, however, those five people help you connect with your intuition, identify areas of your life that may require change, and support you as you give your body what it needs to heal, you will be much less likely to walk around with boxing gloves.

If you don't have friends or family in your life who are able or willing to do this, I have included a Guided Meditation at the end of this chapter to help you. It would be my honor to be your ally in the absence, or even presence, of others.

One of my clients was recently diagnosed with multiple sclerosis (MS) and was seeking coaching to help her achieve a sense of peace. It is relatively common to feel as though the body is attacking or failing us when we face this type of illness, which places us into battle mode.

Exercise has been shown to have multiple beneficial effects on those dealing with MS. She wanted to develop and stick to a plan for physical movement every day, but some days walking down the street felt like moving a mountain. Rather than slipping into the mindset of "my body hates me," we worked on creating a movement vision board. She identified swimming as an activity that she loved.

On days when swimming wasn't physically possible or logically feasible, I encouraged her to do a visualization meditation of participating in the activity. She would imagine herself in a pool that she loves, feeling every breath, arm stroke, and leg movement. Consciously, she knew she wasn't actually swimming, but the visualization reminded her body how much it loved to swim. It allowed her to connect to her body as an ally rather than remain in fight mode.

Your Body Is Your Biggest Fan

Your body doesn't hate you. In fact, it has been your most devoted supporter and dedicated fan since birth. Your heart beats approximately one hundred thousand times a day voluntarily to ensure blood is pumped through each of your organs, delivering the necessary nutrients to perform optimally. You take approximately twenty-two thousand breaths each day without realizing it because your lungs are working tirelessly to fuel the body with oxygen.

Without your help or attention, your liver works to synthesize important proteins, metabolize macromolecules and medications, and detoxify the blood. While you are working and sleeping, your kidneys are busy removing waste products from the body and ensuring your fluids and electrolytes are balanced.

If you feel sick, it's usually a sign that your organs are working in overdrive to help manage the disease. When a microorganism enters your body, your immune system responds by raising your temperature to help you avoid a serious infection. If you suddenly feel nauseous and find yourself miserable in the bathroom, it's often because your body recognized a pathogen in your food or water and is helping you expel it.

Your body is . . . your biggest fan.

Help Them Help You

Your medical team may not support you tirelessly and unconditionally to the extent your body does, but identifying the members of the team as allies will make your journey exponentially more pleasant. In Chapter 1, I reviewed the extreme and rigorous training physicians endure to ultimately help their patients. Most people would not, and honestly could not, complete this without a sincere and genuine inner drive and desire. Keeping this front of mind will help frame your relationship with your physician.

Allies help; enemies hurt. Physicians take the Hippocratic Oath, which is often truncated to "First, do no harm." It is much lengthier in its original form, but it basically states that physicians will abstain from all intentional wrong-doing and causing harm.

Do some physicians take actions and make decisions that harm their patients? Absolutely. Do the vast majority have the intention to harm? Not at all.

Part of establishing a mutually beneficial relationship involves helping your physician collect the necessary information to make the best decisions for your care. If diabetes management is the priority for the next appointment, come prepared with a log of your blood sugar readings and the time each was taken to help the physician evaluate the effectiveness of your current regimen. If you are establishing care with a new physician, bringing your previous medical records and an updated list of your medications is of utmost importance.

In other words, *help them help you.*

And as with any other ally relationship, if you are doing your due diligence, but your physician is not, finding another ally would serve you better than turning that physician into an enemy.

One of my clients asked me to accompany her to a telehealth appointment with a hematologist to evaluate her anemia. He was seeing her for the first time and, like many physicians in this scenario, did not yet have her lab work to review. Expecting this, I was ready to be his ally and had her results ready on my computer to email to him in real time. As a result, he was able to review the areas of concern, develop a treatment plan, and avoid an unnecessary delay due to a lack of information.

Our energy could have been spent being angry at the physician for not obtaining these results in advance. Or angry at the system for dropping the ball yet again. Neither of which would have helped my client receive the care she needed. Instead of making him our enemy, we came prepared to be his ally.

Criticizers Versus Producers

We can either be criticizers or producers. But not both.

As we walk through this life, we identify practices along the way with which we don't agree. Practices that could be done better or changed in some way.

We then find ourselves facing a choice. Either we choose to criticize every aspect of the practice—the creator, the systems, the people managing it, the consumers of it, all of it—or we choose to create something different. A new practice, a new system. A new way of interacting with others on our journey to wellness.

In the first scenario, we are focusing on what's wrong.

In the second, we are changing what's wrong by focusing on what's possible.

I could have spent years of my time criticizing the field of pharmacy, the managers, the systems, the customers. I could also have spent endless time fighting with the three hospital systems that failed to provide optimal care for my dad.

There aren't enough years left in my life to get in all the possible criticism and fighting. So I chose to create instead—create a new way of caring for people. Show them that establishing allies will be more beneficial than creating enemies. And ultimately remind the world that humankind still exists and the path to wellness can be peaceful and beautiful.

I encourage you to create as well. Create a new way of finding peace on this journey.

Peace Points

- When facing a health challenge, seek allies rather than adversaries.
- Your body doesn't hate you; in fact, it's your biggest fan.
- Choose to produce and create rather than criticize and fight.

Guided Meditation

Locate and settle into a comfortable, relatively quiet space. As it feels right, gently close your eyes or gaze softly downward. Begin to connect your senses to the space. Feel the surface beneath you, whether it's a chair, the ground, or otherwise. Notice how gravity is pulling you down onto that surface. Begin to notice the qualities of the air around you. Even notice any close and distance sounds that surround you.

Now begin to connect to your breath. Notice its natural depth and cadence, without judgment. Follow your breath, from the tip of your nostrils down to your lungs and back up with the next exhalation.

Allow the connection to both your physical space and your body's natural breathing pattern to anchor you into the present moment. Return to these anchors as thoughts may begin to take over.

Now imagine the outline of a person in front of you. This person symbolically represents the primary health condition you are facing. Notice any natural tendencies your body may have toward this entity. Are your muscles tightening? Is your breath getting more shallow? Again, no judgment, just awareness. Slowly move your hands towards your knees, palms up as if to receive.

With your palms up, look at this person, this symbol, this entity and ask what message it is trying to send. Try to remain open to receiving this message. Is it here to teach you something? Is it providing a gentle nudge for you to work on a specific lifestyle habit? Is there a relationship in your life that it's focusing on that may need attention or nurturing?

Sit here for a few minutes simply allowing and listening.

Begin to shift your awareness of this image in front of you from an enemy or adversary to an ally, a friend. Imagine it lighting up with love as it shares its message. Imagine it reaching its hands out to yours to offer guidance.

When you feel you are ready, express gratitude to this symbolic messenger for sharing today. Then thank yourself for being open to the message.

As the image retracts, bring your hands to your heart and deepen your breath. Feel the physical space around you again. Know that you can revisit this messenger anytime you need to.

Slowly open your eyes and journal any insights as you wish.

CHAPTER 11

ONWARD

IT seems fitting to end this book on a call to move onward. Toward progress. Toward the future.

Regardless of where you've been in your health journey, there is hope. Hope in finding peace. Hope in unlearning what hasn't served you and relearning what will.

Hope in going *all-in* on your health. Peacefully.

Television and social media often paint a bleak picture of the healthcare system and offer little to no hope. Politicians fight over the idea of socialized medicine. Insurance companies fight for their place in our current landscape. All in an attempt to protect personal interests.

This can leave patients feeling lost in a fight they are too exhausted to participate in.

But I believe in humankind. I see the champions in every medical environment, and I am grateful for them. They want to do the right thing, and their persistence is making a difference, even if on a small scale.

I have spent decades around new and veteran physicians. They give of themselves in ways many of us couldn't imagine. Their genuine desire for those under their care to be healthier versions of themselves is a truth that I can only hope their patients feel.

The Japanese word *kintsugi* literally means "golden joinery," or mending with gold. It is a technique which involves collecting broken ceramic pieces and putting them back together by covering them with real gold. In this way, brokenness and imperfections are not only accepted but become a stronger source of beauty.

Although my father's passing brought an unprecedented level of pain and suffering to my life, it was those emotions that propelled me forward. It was putting those pieces back together that created the beautiful life purpose I later discovered. Had I not lived the healthcare system as a patient's caregiver and witnessed its brokenness first hand, I would lack compassion and empathy for what others experience.

I now know deeply what many of you are facing. I see my dad's face in each of my clients. His journey on earth may be over, but the collective human experience is one I continue to honor.

Instead of hiding or running from the cracks in the healthcare system, I propose we investigate them. Learn from them. Accept them as the current reality, even if we don't approve.

In doing so, we can discover new meaning. New perspectives. And ultimately create beauty out of brokenness.

In a recent article, author Motoki offered an acronym for applying kintsugi to our lives (Motoki 2023).[24] I believe in a similar way, we can apply this acronym to our wellness journey:

K-kindness: Both to others and to ourselves. In practicing self-care and self-compassion, we promote our own healing. This may require an unlearning of the previously connected dots that self-care . . . is selfish. Relearning a healthier perspective on this may look like self-care . . . is both wildly selfless and required for us to give to others out of abundance rather than depletion.

I-investigate: An invitation to investigate our lives. Just as the kintsugi process requires attention to detail, we can investigate and give attention to areas in our life where we need healing. This may not always be the location where our symptoms lie. This investigation must have depth beyond the physical.

---

24   Motoki, "Kintsugi as a Metaphor for Life."

N-notice: You have permission to take the space and time to notice how you feel and what feels off or misaligned. Notice and honor what might be broken.

T-time: The healthcare system didn't break overnight. Similarly, a disease takes time to develop. Healing the system, and ourselves, requires time and patience.

S-stillness: The healing needed at both the system and individual level requires each of us to pause. Get quiet. Silence the external noise. Tune out the societal messaging and find peace.

U-urushii: The Japanese lacquer used in the kintsugi process. Its potency and effectiveness are what create the beautiful restoration. However, it can be extremely harmful in its most pure form. This is parallel to life's duality—some of the most difficult life challenges encourage and promote the best opportunities for healing.

After countless podcast interviews with amazing humans who have been through unspeakable challenges, I have seen and heard firsthand how beauty can and does arise from brokenness.

In our podcast interview, cancer survivor Chris Wark shared, "You need to point your ship toward Healthy Island. Wellness is a destination. That's where you want to be. But you can't just hop on a plane and get there. You have to navigate the ocean. Every day. Things come at you in life. Some days are smooth sailing; some days are really rough and you get knocked off course. But you just have to point your ship toward Healthy Island every day with your choices. Every day, making your way toward your destination."

Every day. *All-in.*

I would like to offer these final Peace Points:

- You have permission to unlearn, relearn, and repeat the process as you feel necessary.

- Physicians and other providers, as a whole, do deeply care for your well-being; they simply need you to partner with them as they do the best they can.

- Your inner guidance can never be replaced by a member of the healthcare system. Check in often with your inner physician.

ACKNOWLEDGMENTS

IT takes a robust village to bring a literary work of passion and purpose to life. Some members of my village are unaware of the role they have played in the development and execution of this book, while others were front and center. All are immensely loved, appreciated, and worthy of acknowledgment beyond what words are able to express.

First and foremost, I want to thank my mom for expressing the deepest, most genuine, unconditional kind of love that exists on this side of the human experience. Her support has been the greatest blessing of my life.

Secondly, but with no lesser significance, I want to thank my husband, Tony. From hearing me share my vision of being a writer many years ago, to encouraging me during the actual process of writing, he has shown unwavering support and love. We have been energetically aligned since high school and now share the beautiful professional experience of elevating the patient journey.

A very special thank you to my son, Dylan, who has consistently reminded me what the pursuit of excellence looks and feels like as he continues to follow his dreams of playing professional soccer.

I'm genuinely grateful to Mrs. Nash, my eighth grade and high school English teacher, who created the initial spark of inspiration that ultimately led to me creating this book. She taught me what passion and purpose in our life's work looks and feels like. As one my biggest cheerleaders back then and now, she played a significant role in helping me bring this book to life.

To my business mentors, Jadah Sellner and Giovanni Marsico, thank you for encouraging me to hold a vision for myself and my impact on this world that far exceeds my current ability to see. You have rewired my brain to think limitlessly, imaginatively, and with a hyperfocus on becoming the person who can radically change the healthcare landscape for the better.

To my previous pharmacy leader, Guy DiPasqua, thank you for always leading with a servant heart and creating a loving energetic space for me to dream bigger.

Finally, and with a full heart, I want to express my eternal gratitude to my past, present, and future clients. Your willingness to trust me and allow me to take your hand as we walk together on this journey is the most beautiful honor of my lifetime.

REFERENCES

Bolton, Derek. 2020. "The Biopsychosocial Model and the New Medical Humanism." *Archives de Philosophie* 83 (4): 13–40. https://www. cairn-int.info/article-E_APHI_834_0013--the-biopsychosocial-model-and-the-new.htm.

Canale, Stefano Del, Daniel Z. Louis, Vittorio Maio, Xiaohong Wang, Giuseppina Rossi, Mohammadreza Hojat, and Joseph S. Gonnella. 2012. "The Relationship between Physician Empathy and Disease Complications." *Academic Medicine* 87 (9): 1243–49. https://doi. org/10.1097/acm.0b013e3182628fbf.

Chen, Pin-Hao A., Jin Hyun Cheong, Eshin Jolly, Hirsh Elhence, Tor D. Wager, and Luke J. Chang. 2019. "Socially Transmitted Placebo Effects." *Nature Human Behaviour* 3 (12): 1295–1305. https://doi. org/10.1038/s41562-019-0749-5.

Crowley, Jennifer, Lauren Ball, and Gerrit Jan Hiddink. 2019. "Nutrition in Medical Education: A Systematic Review." *The Lancet Planetary Health* 3 (9): e379–89. https://doi.org/10.1016/ s2542-5196(19)30171-8.

Custers, Eugène J.F.M., and Olle ten Cate. 2018. "The History of Medical Education in Europe and the United States, with Respect to Time and Proficiency." *Academic Medicine* 93 (3S): S49–54. https://doi.org/10.1097/acm.0000000000002079.

"FDA at a GLANCE REGULATED PRODUCTS and FACILITIES." 2021. https://www.fda.gov/media/154548/download.

Holt-Lunstad, Julianne, Timothy B. Smith, and J. Bradley Layton. 2010. "Social Relationships and Mortality Risk: A Meta-Analytic Review." Edited by Carol Brayne. *PLoS Medicine* 7 (7). https://doi.org/10.1371/journal.pmed.1000316.

House, J., K. Landis, and D Umberson. 1988. "Social Relationships and Health." *Science* 241 (4865): 540–45. https://doi.org/10.1126/science.3399889.

Hulail, Mohey. 2018. "Humanism in Medical Practice: What, Why and How?" *Hos Pal Med Int Jnl* 2 (6): 336–39. https://doi.org/10.15406/hpmij.2018.02.00119.

Katie, Byron. 2021. *LOVING WHAT IS : Four Questions That Can Change Your Life.* S.L.: Harmony Crown.

Lelorain, Sophie, Anne Brédart, Sylvie Dolbeault, and Serge Sultan. 2012. "A Systematic Review of the Associations Between Empathy Measures and Patient Outcomes in Cancer Care." *Psycho-Oncology* 21 (12): 1255–64. https://doi.org/10.1002/pon.2115.

Liddy, C. 2020. "How Long Are Canadians Waiting to Access Specialty Care?" *Can Fam Physician* 66 (6): 434–44.

Merck. 2018. "State of Curiosity Report." 2018.

https://www.emdgroup.com/company/us/State-of-Curiosity-Report-2018-USA-CAN.pdf.

Moseley, George. 2008. "The U.S. Health Care Non-System, 1908–2008." *AMA Journal of Ethics* 10 (5): 324–31. https://doi.org/10.1001/virtualmentor.2008.10.5.mhst1-0805.

Motoki. 2023. "Kintsugi as a Metaphor for Life." Medium. April 12, 2023. https://medium.com/-motoki/kintsugi-as-a-metaphor-for-life-9f79d3b24ad3.

NORC. 2021. "Surveys of Trust in the U.S. Health Care System." 2021. www.norc.org. May 21, 2021. https://www.norc.org/PDFs/ABIM%20Foundation/20210520_NORC_ABIM_Foundation_Trust%20in%20Healthcare_Part%201.pdf.

Peters, Michele, Caroline M. Potter, Laura Kelly, and Ray Fitzpatrick. 2019. "Self-Efficacy and Health-Related Quality of Life: A Cross-Sectional Study of Primary Care Patients with Multi-Morbidity." *Health and Quality of Life Outcomes* 17 (1). https://doi.org/10.1186/s12955-019-1103-3.

Rakel, David, Bruce Barrett, Zhengjun Zhang, Theresa Hoeft, Betty Chewning, Lucille Marchand, and Jo Scheder. 2011. "Perception of Empathy in the Therapeutic Encounter: Effects on the Common Cold." *Patient Education and Counseling* 85 (3): 390–97. https://doi.org/10.1016/j.pec.2011.01.009.

Rankin, Lissa. 2020. *Mind over Medicine: Scientific Proof That You Can Heal Yourself*. Carlsbad, California: Hay House, Inc.

Rodziewicz, Thomas L, John E Hipskind, and Benjamin Houseman. 2022. "Medical Error Reduction and Prevention." National Library of Medicine. StatPearls Publishing. 2022. https://www.ncbi.nlm.nih.gov/books/NBK499956/.

"The Arnold P. Gold Foundation." n.d. The Arnold P. Gold Foundation. Accessed April 5, 2023. https://www.gold-foundation.org.

Trostle, James A. 1997. "The History and Meaning of Patient Compliance as an Ideology." *Handbook of Health Behavior Research II*, 109–24. https://doi.org/10.1007/978-1-4899-1760-7_6.

Valtorta, Nicole K, Mona Kanaan, Simon Gilbody, Sara Ronzi, and Barbara Hanratty. 2016. "Loneliness and Social Isolation as Risk Factors for Coronary Heart Disease and Stroke: Systematic Review and Meta-Analysis of Longitudinal Observational Studies." *Heart* 102 (13): 1009–16. https://doi.org/10.1136/heartjnl-2015-308790.

Van Bulck, Liesbet, Koen Luyckx, Eva Goossens, Leen Oris, and Philip Moons. 2018. "Illness Identity: Capturing the Influence of Illness on the Person's Sense of Self." *European Journal of Cardiovascular Nursing* 18 (1): 4–6. https://doi.org/10.1177/1474515118811960.